ARCHITOURISM

ARCHITOURISM
AUTHENTIC
ESCAPIST
EXOTIC
SPECTACULAR

EDITED BY
JOAN OCKMAN
AND
SALOMON FRAUSTO

DESIGNED BY
BRETT SNYDER

ARCHITOURISM
AUTHENTIC
ESCAPIST
EXOTIC
SPECTACULAR

**A BUELL CENTER /
COLUMBIA BOOK OF ARCHITECTURE**

PRESTEL
MUNICH BERLIN LONDON NEW YORK

POINT OF DEPARTURE

This volume is based on a conference and exhibition entitled
Architourism: Architecture as a Destination for Tourism, organized in
2002 by the Temple Hoyne Buell Center for the Study of American
Architecture at Columbia University. Its immediate provocation was
the "Bilbao effect." One of the architectural surprises of the end of the
last century was undoubtedly the spectacular success of Frank
Gehry's Guggenheim Museum in Bilbao, completed in 1997. That a
singular building in a provincial locale could so captivate the popular
imagination, globally and locally, highbrow and low-, seemed
remarkable. That it should be credited with regenerating a whole city
at a time when bricks and mortar (even glass and titanium) had
supposedly been displaced by lighter and faster forms of cultural
currency was reason for celebrating—at least among architects—
as much as for reflection.

We began planning *Architourism* back in 2000. After September 2001, in the context of the intense debates over the rebuilding of Ground Zero in New York, the issues seemed no less relevant, even if the optimism of Bilbao was now tempered by a new focus on memorialization and what Lucy Lippard calls in her essay in this volume "tragic tourism." Among the questions we initially wished to pose was what, if anything, was different about this contemporary architectural "effect" from that produced by earlier historical monuments. How do the new pilgrimage sites differ from the Taj Mahal and the Alhambra, the Crystal Palace and the Eiffel Tower, or for that matter twentieth-century buildings like the Sydney Opera House and the Pompidou Center? In what ways have contemporary media culture, globalization, urbanism, and twenty-first-century economics changed the relationship between architecture and tourism?

We coined the term *architourism* by analogy to other types of tourism like ecotourism, art tourism, and heritage tourism, in order to suggest that architecture, in becoming a marketable destination today, now has its own niche in the tourist industry. Is this a passing fashion or destined to last? Will architourism, as Mitchell Schwarzer wonders in his opening essay in this book, stimulate the creation of any lasting masterpieces?

We were also interested in exploring some forms of "desire" that motivate this type of tourism. We thus organized the conference around four categories: *Authentic, Exotic, Escapist,* and *Spectacular.* We have preserved that structure in the present volume. At the exhibition, rather than display a selection of architect-designed "architourist" buildings, we chose to invite a group of artists and architects to present projects that reflected on the issues in critical or speculative ways. This work is interspersed throughout on the yellow "site-seer" pages. One project, Hans Haacke's commemorative poster for the World Trade Center, has been specially reformatted as an insert (see after page 80).

Examples of architourist architecture also abound throughout the book. The *Spectacular* section features three of them—one, a temporary structure built for an international exposition in Switzerland by Diller + Scofidio; one, an unbuilt project for Paris by Bernard Tschumi Architects; and the third and largest, currently under construction in Guadalajara, Mexico, master-planned by TEN Arquitectos. A few "detours," appearing on pink pages, glance at very recent projects planned or built around the world, and suggest some vicissitudes of the architourist strategy today.

Thousands of people watch the fireworks display in front of Santiago de Compostela's cathedral on the eve of the feast day of Santiago, the patron saint of the northwestern Spanish region of Galicia, 2001. Photo: EFE, Lavandeira Jr., AP Photo

Although the field of tourist studies is by now well established, architecture has only recently begun to enter into its discourse as a major focus. We wish to acknowledge the seminal writings of Dean MacCannell, who took part in the conference and whose work has been generally inspirational for this project. A recent book edited by D. Medina Lasansky, a contributor to this volume, and Brian McLaren, *Architecture and Tourism: Perception, Performance and Place* (Berg, 2004), represents a noteworthy addition to the literature.

Along with those whose work is represented in this book, many people lent their insights, talents, and resources to the different components of the project. We wish to acknowledge the Graduate School of Architecture, Planning and Preservation at Columbia and its former dean, Bernard Tschumi, for generously supporting the conference and exhibition. Our appreciation goes to Marina Urbach for curatorial and organizational assistance; to Evan Douglis, with the assistance of Richard Sarrach, for a vivid exhibition design and installation; to Chris Barker, Willi Kunz, and Pedro Pachano for production help; to Muna Tseng for so kindly making available the work of Tseng Kwong Chi; and to Herbert Muschamp for agreeing to substitute for Jon Jerde in the *Escapist* session of the conference on very short notice. We are especially grateful to Martha Rosler (whose photography also appears in this book) for a spectacular poster design. For their collaboration on this book, we owe major thanks to Stephanie Salomon and Zoë Slutzky for copyediting and Sara Goldsmith for research assistance. For a truly dazzling book design, we are deeply indebted to Brett Snyder. Our good friend Angeli Sachs welcomed this book at Prestel; our sincere gratitude to her and also to Sandra Leitte and Matthias Hauer.

This book offers a rich variety of perspectives on a significant phenomenon of our time. If, as Yi-Fu Tuan suggests, great architecture continues to offer the most direct route out of our mundane experience, it will continue to be a destination for twenty-first-century pilgrims, even in this jaded age of spectacle and hype.

JOAN OCKMAN AND SALOMON FRAUSTO
APRIL 2005

MITCHELL SCHWARZER
ARCHITECTURE AND MASS TOURISM

The message on my room telephone instructed me to meet the group at eight-thirty the next morning in the lobby of the Jinling Hotel. It was my first visit to Beijing and I had signed up for an all-day tour of the Forbidden City and Summer Palace. When I got downstairs I easily made out the group gathered around Lee, the tour guide, who was wearing an orange knit shirt and holding up a small red flag. There were sixteen of us and we waded through perfunctory introductions. After a few minutes, as the huge bus awkwardly floated out of the parking lot, we were on our way. Although fantastic sights were in store, I also had another agenda. I wanted to understand better the relationship between mass tourism and architectural monuments. How is a great building seen from the vantage point of a package tour? What kind of knowledge is gained? What happens when mass-market commerce and the upper echelon of architecture intersect?

That particular morning a leaden sky promised cool weather, perfect for sightseeing. Our route took us down Chang-an Avenue toward the heart of the Chinese capital. We cut through a cityscape of crushingly large buildings. Since the 1990s, Beijing has been in the throes of a nonstop boom. Practically every block sported one or two construction cranes and trays of bamboo scaffolding. Ten years ago, most of these buildings didn't exist. I gazed out of the window intoxicated by the breadth and scope of development. Never in all my travels had I encountered even a fraction of this clamor of construction.

Tourists pose at the Forbidden City in Beijing, 2003. Photo: Greg Baker, AP Photo

Strangely, during the entire drive, which lasted forty-five minutes, Lee never mentioned the elusive scene passing by. He began lecturing us about emperors and dynasties. After twenty minutes, though, his words began to blur together. Noticing the rows of drooping eyes, Lee abruptly switched to contemporary life, and peppered the air with anecdotes on the size of his kitchen and the price of his car. A bright, engaging man, Lee knew the secret of the package tour. Shower the customers first with the colossal, and when their faces are dripping with wonder and looking a wee bit tired, freshen them up with tidbits of local color that resonate with their lives back home. Tour guides worldwide accommodate the tourist's lack of familiarity with a locale by weaving between the grand and the everyday. Although tourist attention is captured by the abnormalities of scale and the grotesqueries of ornament, it needs periodic moments of the mundane for rest and relaxation.

A military police officer patrols Tiananmen Square in Beijing, 1999. Photo: Chien-min Chung, AP Photo

We got off the bus a considerable distance from the entrance to the Forbidden City, since Lee intended to steer us through Tiananmen Square and its gauntlet of vendors. The rest and relaxation demanded by the tourist manifests itself frequently in shopping opportunities, and Chinese architectural sites abound in souvenirs—a miniature of a building, a silk-screened kerchief emblazoned with a pagoda roof, t-shirts, hats, and other articles of clothing mixing Chinese characters and dragons. The reproductions themselves don't matter all that much, since most of them are poorly executed. More critical is the diversion of shopping alongside a famous monument. Exposed to unfamiliar histories and surrounded by exhausting spaces, tourists crave the familiar. For a few moments we slip back into routines of acquisition we have known since childhood. The small clay emperors and little metal objects my companions purchased outside the Forbidden City brought the awe-inspiring architectural site into their hands and shoulder bags.

Souvenirs have another longer-term purpose. After the trip, they will join others to record, in tangible form, the extraordinary moments of a person's life. As Lucy Lippard comments in *On the Beaten Track* (1999), all types of bought, found, and given souvenirs become the touchstones through which people make sense of their lives.[1] Arranged on walls, desktops, and mantels, souvenirs pack a place with travel memories. At least for their purchaser, they connect the monumental architecture of the trip with the architecture of home. Watching television or conversing with family, one has only to glance at a figurine or trinket to find the room illuminated with the pungent peculiarity of the faraway.

Other than shopping, our group's main activity in Tiananmen Square consisted of snapping photographs, yet another tourist abstraction of architecture. Time and again, against a backdrop of long walls and high towers, the cameras clicked furiously. These were once-in-a-lifetime sights. They had to be captured or else the experience would be lost. The cumulative time spent photographing left little time for direct encounters. No matter, for the tour members the lens and reproduced image were a valued substitute. In The *Tourist Gaze* (1990), John Urry writes of the search for photo opportunities: "Tourist agencies spend much time indicating where photographs should be taken (so-called viewing points). Indeed much tourism becomes in effect a search for the photogenic; travel is a strategy for the accumulation of photographs."[2]

Returning from a trip, I hear the question, "Do you have photographs?" far more often than "Do you have stories or observations?" When I came home from China and had my rolls of film developed, my wife was thrilled to see an image of me perched on a stretch of the Great Wall. "It really exists," she exclaimed, "Look, you're standing on it." Seeing me at the Wall in a photograph validated my trip, as well as the existence of the Wall. Countless photographs had first familiarized the monument. Now, a single photograph personalized it. When I showed a friend a different photograph of me at another section of the Wall he was confused. "That's the Wall?" The problem with this second photo was that it wasn't taken at Badaling, where the first image was snapped. Instead of the familiar, restored section of Wall, it showed a stretch of irregular rocks that could be mistaken for many places. I had to

explain that most of the Great Wall isn't so great, that it looks in fact like this ruined section. I added that the ruined section is fascinating, but my friend had already moved on; or rather back in the photo album, to look once more at the Great Wall at Badaling.

I've often noticed that tourists need something more than a building to anchor a photograph. For a large structure, whose size and dimensions can barely be captured in even a series of photographs, a sign outside will accomplish the purpose. The sign names the building, dates it, and sometimes tells a bit of its history. During my group tour to Tiananmen Square, Mao's giant portrait above the gate to the Forbidden City had the desired effect. Regardless of the Chairman's incongruity with the Imperial past or capitalist present, his image branded the site. It was as if the long walls of architecture were under a shadow of obscurity, until the great face of celebrity cast a light of recognition—something Andy Warhol would have appreciated.

Our visit to the Forbidden City ended up lasting a little over an hour. The group tour is highly prescriptive. No matter how intricate a building's spaces, the tour moves along the same paths worn by thousands of other groups. Amid the many thousands of visitors that day, I felt like a calf at a roundup. Lee moved us with the skill of a youthful cowboy, herding the body of the group over and over again to a desired viewing pen and lassoing the strays, like myself, when we ventured too far. At each stop, his voice filled the air with facts. As I would be staring at a column detail or the vista of the grand axis, I couldn't help but hear his words, and, for that matter, those of other guided tours giving what must have been the

Chinese tourists climb the Great Wall at Badaling near Beijing, 2004. Photo: Ng Han Guan, AP Photo

same spiel in a smorgasbord of languages. Listening, I realized that practically none of the guides, including Lee, had much to say about the Forbidden City's architectural ideas. The focus was on eminent persons, scandalous events, and valuable furnishings. Lee delighted in telling us the cost of things or the number of rooms or bathrooms. He had no comments about a building's structure, program, and detail, or a compound's circulation and spaces. That day, I couldn't move at my own pace; I couldn't look at anything with even a modicum of silence; and I didn't gain much architectural information.

The group tour can feel like a forced march. Because tourists from developed countries take relatively short vacations and have considerable financial resources, the pressure is on to pack it in. Brochures list monuments like courses at a banquet, items to be delicately savored. In reality, the tour devours architecture, clicking off sites as quickly as a wolf eats its kill. Each year, more and more tourists take quick airplane hops, waking at dawn and knocking off an isolated architectural monument before it's time to fly back and have lunch. Companies make sure that travel proceeds efficiently and time isn't squandered. Tour companies, and, for that matter, most entertainment venues nowadays, loathe empty minutes. We must be occupied. I have only an indistinct memory of how imposing the Forbidden City was, for I never had the luxury of letting my feet and eyes wander through its forbidding spaces. We kept moving. Maybe Lee didn't want us to get bored, or maybe he wanted to maximize our photo and shopping opportunities.

Thoughts of this kind stirred in my head as we exited the Forbidden City's northern gate and were accosted by yet another phalanx of vendors. We were on our way to lunch and then a drive on Beijing's expressways to the Summer Palace used by the emperors. En route the bus made an unadvertised stop at a factory producing porcelain plates and figures, with an adjoining and far larger store selling these items and every other conceivable knickknack. I drifted outside and sat on an uncomfortable brick wall for almost an hour, angry that I had to waste my time this way and knowing quite well, by looking at my watch, that our time at the Summer Palace would be rushed. I gloomily pondered whether the mass tour was some sort of mass deception, a couple of short visits to marvelous buildings surrounded by untold hours of consumption. But perhaps the glass was half full. Sitting there, alongside one of Beijing's ubiquitous rattling construction sites, I began to reflect on the fact that our group had just visited (and was about to visit) places that had always been off-limits. Monuments like the Forbidden City or Summer Palace—or for that matter, the pyramids of Mexico, the churches of medieval Europe, and the Buddhist temples of Japan—had been built with no thought of mass tourism. They had all been exclusive, with visits limited to selected castes of people at selective hours. They have now found a new purpose: the entertainment and edification of the masses. Because of modern transportation and improved public access, the masterpieces of world architecture have come within the grasp of hundreds of millions of people. I began to realize that my companions, then busily shopping, were visiting on this day places of extraordinary power. The mass tour, for all its flaws, allowed us to cross the threshold of buildings that most people in previous centuries couldn't have dreamed of entering.

Back at the hotel, looking over various Beijing tour brochures, I noticed two basic types of tours. The first, the majority of excursions, took in the famed sights—the Great Wall, the Temple of Heaven, the Summer Palace, and the Forbidden City. These destinations consisted of historical structures of considerable age, unusual form, and exceptional size. But even more important, they were places to which tourists had been exposed before their trip. They are documented extensively in guidebooks, illustrated in coffee-table volumes and travel magazines, and featured on the Discovery or Travel channels. The great architectural sights are the displayed and advertised sights, those long ago turned into photographs, film, or video, those transported from fixed places into portable and multiple lives as imagery.

The second type of tour covers more obscure sites that appeal to our quest for quaintness. In Beijing the old courtyard houses, known as *hutong,* fit the bill. While throughout China these districts (composed of one-story structures) are being demolished to make way for high-rises, in a few selected places—whose diminishing number the Chinese tourist agencies will undoubtedly regret with time—provision is made to showcase "old" China. Instead of wandering on their own, however, the vast majority of tourists see the *hutong* district from the backseat of a pedicab. Perhaps unguided they would get lost in the labyrinth of crooked streets or perhaps they wouldn't know to enter the charming mom-and-pop artisan houses and sample their tales, foods, and crafts. To my way of thinking, far from being an exploration of genuine Chinese life, these stuffed buildings substitute an all-too-familiar global quaintness for the gritty reality of high-rise Chinese domesticity. Yet it is unlikely that these otherwise economically infeasible districts would be preserved without mass tourism. A few isolated tourists poking about, like myself, couldn't accomplish this act of preservation. It takes an army of tourists to save a village.

In between the picturesque and the overpowering there really wasn't any advertised architecture to tour. I couldn't find any excursions to lesser-known antiquities, early Western-influenced architecture, or the Socialist Realism of the Maoist era. As elsewhere in the world, tour buses speed past the bulk of Chinese architecture without a notice. In Beijing, I ended up wandering alone for days, only encountering large numbers of tourists as I approached the sanctioned sites.

Looking back, I realize that I signed up for the day tour because it was a convenient way to visit far-flung sites within an unfamiliar metropolis. Several of my companions, all Americans, and all apparently affluent and highly educated, told me they booked the tour for similar reasons. Why then weren't they as bothered by the tour's pace and priorities? Part of the answer lies in the fact that none of them work in the fields of architecture or art. They were businesswomen, doctors, lawyers, and university professors. They probably don't reflect much on architecture in their daily lives, and therefore appreciated whatever information they got from Lee. Visiting architectural monuments was a leisure-time activity that fit well with photographing, strolling, shopping, and dining. For the mass tourist, architecture might be the entrée for a trip, but in the end it is just one course out of a long menu.

A tourist takes a souvenir photo in front of the haze-covered Petronas Twin Towers, completed in 1998 to a design by Cesar Pelli, in downtown Kuala Lumpur, Malaysia, 2004. Photo: Teh Eng Koon, AP Photo

TOURING MODERN AND CONTEMPORARY ARCHITECTURE

Nowadays, large swaths of cities around the world fall to the tourist. These districts' rhythms follow the comings and goings of buses, boats, trains, and planes. A tourist precinct is in some ways less a part of its own region than a point along the international lanes of travel. In summertime especially the number of tourists can approximate or exceed the number of locals. It is common to run into people one has met a few days earlier at another attraction. Tourist-overrun Venice, in this sense, relates less to the nearby Veneto than to other Italian tourist centers like Florence.

When it comes to old monuments, the gap between the tourist zone and local culture can become as wide as the Grand Canyon. Most tours to Greece concentrate on sunny islands and ivory columns dating back to classical times. Many tourists are surprised when, and if, they find out that modern Greece grew out of Roman/Byzantine civilization and Christianity. I remember traveling in Egypt one winter and realizing that the places my wife and I were visiting—the various pyramids near Cairo, and Thebes and Luxor, Aswan, and Abu Simbel— constituted an alternative Egypt. Several Egyptians I spoke to avoided the tourist districts and pharaonic monuments, remarking that they did not represent the reality of Islamic Egypt but a cruel Western perversion of it. Like the pilgrimage routes of medieval times, whose churches and towns acquired a common appearance, today's great tourist architecture— from the Parthenon to the Temple of Karnak—unfolds against a linear trail, isolated from the wider cultures it cuts through. The postcards say it all. They catalogue the sights not to be missed. Perhaps that is why the buildings and places that don't appear in gift shops are shrouded in obscurity.

Works of modern architecture customarily have been left off the postcards, and out of the tours and the guidebooks. In part because of its assault on tradition, the great works of the modern movement have rarely been included in mass tours premised on tradition. I learned years ago that guidebooks of all stripes—from the *Blue Guide* to the *Lonely Planet*— omitted the accomplishments of architecture after the year 1900. With rare exceptions, the focus was on older, preindustrial monuments. Even famous works by Mies van der Rohe, Louis Kahn, or Tadao Ando often merit no mention. The only recourse is to find a specific architectural guide or compose an architectural tour of one's own through extensive research beforehand.

Modern architecture's neglect by mass tourism does offer some enticing opportunities for intrepid individuals. To take the modern equivalent of the aristocratic Grand Tour, and leisurely ramble amid glorious and deserted buildings, all one has to do is locate a couple of twentieth-century masterpieces and traverse the city space or countryside between them. Like most architectural historians, I've visited hundreds of such buildings and usually had the sites to myself. A few of the most famous buildings accommodate the public on tours or provide hours for individual viewing. In the most renowned, like Le Corbusier's Villa Savoye or chapel at Ronchamp, there is usually a small crowd, which, upon closer inspection, consists largely of skinny black-clothed architects and architectural students.

Tourists on camels ride past the Chephren Pyramid on Egypt's Giza Plateau,1995. Photo: Mohamed El-Dakhakhny, AP Photo

On my visits to other famed buildings, like Walter Gropius's Fagus Factory in Germany or Oscar Niemeyer's Ministry of Education and Health in Rio de Janeiro, I didn't see another visitor in hours of touring. It is also the case that many modernist landmarks have limited public access, if any at all. Since our impressions of famous buildings are so conditioned by famous photographs, I have made it my business to see the archetypal views. In Palm Springs, after walking back and forth on the residential road alongside Richard Neutra's Kaufmann House and catching only a view of the front entrance, I noticed some workers slipping onto the property through a hedgerow. When I followed them through the bushes I found myself facing the house in almost exactly the same position used by Julius Shulman in his 1947 photograph. In order to remain on that spot for more than a few seconds I had to feign interest in the workers' project of renovating a wall next to the swimming pool. In Vienna, buying time for a gaze at the rear facade of Adolf Loos's Steiner House was much harder. I easily reached the backyard, but in order to remain there I had to undergo the threats of a resident, who, screaming from her third-story window, repeatedly assured me she would have me arrested for trespassing.

There has to be an easier way. Many cities have capitalized on the audience for organized tours of modern architecture. Chicago hosts numerous excursions through the city's

Santiago Calatrava, Milwaukee Art Museum, 1994–2000.

canyons of tall buildings and lanes of Prairie-style houses. In my own city of Oakland, California, there are walking tours that focus on modern apartment-building design along Lake Merritt or midcentury ranch houses in the foothills. While such efforts go a long way to broaden exposure to modern architecture, they only rarely accommodate large numbers of tourists. Mass tourism, the kind that has demonstrable economic impacts on a city, depends on a media buzz.

Of late, a new word, *architourism*, unveils the possibility for a single work of contemporary (or modern) architecture by a name architect to attract hordes of tourists to a previously marginal place. In 1997, the opening of Frank Gehry's Guggenheim Museum in northern Spain inaugurated what has been called the "Bilbao effect." Tour groups and individuals who wouldn't have given a second's thought to visiting the gritty industrial city of Bilbao descended in droves. The acclaimed building brought economic vitality to the region, generating hundreds of millions of dollars in its first three years. One can now view the Spanish city's aging steel mills and shipyards from the sidewalk tables of a glitzy restaurant and then shop in one of many designer boutiques. In Milwaukee, Wisconsin, another new museum has sparked life into yet another grimy industrial city. The Milwaukee Art Museum by Santiago Calatrava, completed in 2001, successfully transplanted the Bilbao effect to the shores of Lake Michigan, attracting a half million visitors during its first year. On a smaller scale, in 2004, the small northern California city of Redding unveiled a footbridge by Calatrava. Spanning the upper Sacramento River, the soaring Sundial Bridge has lured thousands of people to exit the Interstate and venture into the largely unknown former cow town, turning it into a tourist stopover.

The marketing principles behind architourism are also being applied to older works of modern architecture. In 2002, in Bartlesville, Oklahoma, the Price Tower Art Center opened—a repackaging of Frank Lloyd Wright's landmark Price Tower as a major destination. Attendance climbed 80 percent over the previous year as crowds flocked to visit the building, with its new inn, shops, and restaurant. In 2003, the center announced plans to construct an addition by Zaha Hadid, which would be the world-renowned architect's second building in North America. The addition is already being advertised on the Price Tower Art Center's Web site as "the next landmark." Finally, interest in Wright is writ so large that in 2004 several projects were announced in Buffalo, New York, to create "authentic" Wright buildings from the architect's plans. The unabashed goal of the gas station, boathouse, and cemetery designs is to draw tourists to the area, along the lines of Wright's famous house at Fallingwater, which, even in its remote rural location in Pennsylvania, counts 100,000 visitors a year.

As of my visit to Beijing in 2004, architourism had not yet reached the Chinese mainland. But that seems destined to change. Several eye-popping buildings by star architects are under construction. Just behind the Maoist-era Great Hall of the People on Tiananmen Square rises the new National Grand Theater housing the Beijing Opera. Designed by French architect Paul Andreu, the elliptical titanium dome has been described as " a pearl on a lake." (In this case, there is no lake. The lake is the city.) When I climbed to the

summit of Renmin Park one day to take in the view of the Forbidden City, Andreu's structure looked more like an alien metallic eggshell hatched from the bosom of China's cosmic-scale tourist ambitions.

Down the street from my Beijing hotel I could see the site for the new headquarters for Central Chinese Television (CCTV), designed by Rem Koolhaas. The CCTV Tower will be one of the most audacious skyscrapers ever built, a continuous loop of vertical and horizontal slabs. In a city of hundreds of gigantic buildings competing for attention, Koolhaas's might just have the stuff to stand out as a contemporary icon.

For now, Hong Kong presents the best tourist show of contemporary Chinese architecture—one that is featured in newspaper travel sections worldwide. In the Tsim Sha Tsui district of Kowloon, the waterfront promenade—the Avenue of the Stars—showcases not only Hong Kong cinema under one's feet but also Hong Kong building in the sky. Across the narrow channel, it is easy to see the tall buildings climbing up the island's mountains, striping the green slopes with walls of glass and concrete hundreds of feet high and thousands of feet long. At night, a group of the tallest buildings in the city's Central District participates in a sound-and-light show. Loudspeakers along the walkway announce the extravaganza. To the tunes of symphonic music and epic narration we are taken on a skyline tour. Twenty different buildings are named, each individually identified by flashing lights or lasers. Two architects are mentioned: the Hong Kong and Shanghai Bank's Norman Foster, and the Bank of China's I. M. Pei. Then, while the narrator rhapsodizes about Hong Kong's energetic economy and brilliant future, the buildings shed their staid financial selves and try to convince us we've entered a razzle-dazzle Las Vegas by the South China Sea. For twenty minutes, the tall buildings turn into signs, vibrating bands of light, and flaming incandescent colors, soaring into the sky on projecting laser beams. Unlike most sound-and-light shows aimed at bringing a historical stone monument alive, this object theater by the harbor launches the architecture of Hong Kong into a giddy futurism.

As shown by the examples of Beijing and Hong Kong, architourism is not confined to marginal cities. Large cities around the world have become aware that striking buildings by signature architects can act as touristic cash cows. In recent years, Koolhaas's library in Seattle, Gehry's Disney Concert Hall in Los Angeles, and Herzog & do Meuron's Tate Modern in London function in this way; each has been lauded for invigorating a previously sleepy urban district. Stunning new architecture can even draw tourists to the most remote parts of the globe. The recent Tjibaou Cultural Center by Renzo Piano has put the city of Noumea, New Caledonia, on the tourist map—one tour Web site touts it as one of the next Seven Wonders of the World.

Using a building to stimulate tourism and solidify urban identity is hardly a new phenomenon, having a history dating back to ancient Greece. In modern times, landmark skyscrapers have been the boldest signatures of urban identity, attracting tremendous

Frank Gehry, Guggenheim Museum Bilbao, Spain, 1997. Photo: Eugene Pons. Reprinted from Aurora Cuito, *Guggenheim* (2001)

numbers of tourists. On a slightly more modest scale, particular concert halls, museums, bridges, or monuments have stood out from their surroundings and lent their cities the glamour of instant recognition and allure. In the period preceding the rise of architourism, Eero Saarinen's Gateway Arch in St. Louis (1966) and Jørn Utzon's Sydney Opera House (1973) became icons of their respective cities, drawing millions of visitors over the years. The difference today lies in the number of tourist-magnet buildings underway, as well as the global marketing considerations that go into all aspects of project planning, including design. Tourism is a far more important sector of the world economy than it was fifty or one hundred years ago.

What makes Gehry's Guggenheim Museum Bilbao and Calatrava's Milwaukee Art Museum unique in their settings, and the reason they were chosen from among other possible designs, is their iconoclastic form. At the time of their construction they looked like no other architecture. This exceptionality accords well with the mechanics of mass tourism. Tour groups greedily consume one-of-a-kind things. The planners for both museums were aware of this fact, and, in formulating the projects, consciously associated visual spectacle with income streams. Once, each city relied on a specific confluence of raw materials, transportation routes, and labor to generate industrial revenue; now, each relies on a different confluence of architectural fantasy, slightly different transportation routes, and tourists to generate entertainment revenue.

Office for Metropolitan Architecture, CCTV Tower, Beijing, 2002.

It has helped that both buildings photograph well. Their size and complexity can be captured in a single immediately identifiable shot. Such reductive image-bites are employed in a variety of sales campaigns—from billboards to postcards, brochures, magazine spreads, and the Internet. As Briavel Holcomb points out in his essay "Marketing Cities for Tourism" (1999), in the tourist realm "it is the consumer, not the product, that moves. Because the product is usually sold before the consumer sees it, the marking of tourism is intrinsically more significant than in the conventional case where the product can be seen, tested, and compared to similar products *in situ*. It means that the representation of place, the images created for marketing, the vivid videos and persuasive prose of advertising texts, can be as selective and creative as the marketer can make them—a reality check comes only after arrival."[3]

Increasingly, the kind of contemporary architecture that stimulates mass tourism has to be not only photogenic but also telegenic—buildings that look striking in a sequence of rapid-fire cuts or that stand out in a static shot behind the pretty features of a talking head. Many buildings of this sort end up as backdrops. It is easy to imagine that at the 2008 Olympics in Beijing, correspondents will line up to deliver their reports in front of the National Swimming Center. Even before ground was broken, the "Water Cube," by the Australian firm PTW, had been deemed historic. The fact that underwater bubbles inspired the facade design will no doubt suffuse media descriptions and contribute to lasting audience appeal. It will be fascinating to see how the cameras choose between Beijing's old monuments and the new line of architectural eye candy.

A THEORY OF TOURIST PERCEPTION

Does architourism have anything in common with its linguistic progenitor, ecotourism? Born in the 1980s, ecotourism defines a mode of tourism in which a holiday in the sun is accompanied by a large and oftentimes sobering dose of environmental awareness. Ecology shifts our understanding from the singular to the system. Instead of being shown a few precious sites, ecotourists learn about biodiversity, the myriad and often mundane parts that make up the complete context of an environment. Ecotourism also emphasizes the preservation of the environment through the creation of clean tourist industries, economies that can support the indigenous communities of a region minus the destructive effects of logging or mining. Similarly, cultural tourism initiates visitors into the less visible and obvious layers of a place. Here, buildings are experienced not just for their aesthetic attributes or status within architectural history. What counts most is their ability to conjure up the disparate pieces of community.

Despite claims for authenticity, ecotourism and cultural tourism can only bring tourists so far into a natural or historical environment; local residents would not want such enterprises to be more intrusive. Still, within their limits, these modes of organized tourism encourage a more thoughtful sort of visit. The geography covered tends to be smaller and the history uncovered tends to be deeper. It is worth pondering whether there can be an urban version of eco- and cultural tourism, a journey into the heart or limbs of a metropolis with the intent of raising important issues—like sustainability, waste pollution, suburban sprawl, the destruction of old built fabric.

Yet it is hard to correlate mass tourism's monument hopping, even if it includes contemporary as well as older buildings, with environmental and cultural education. Architourism seems to be more like the emotive side of ecotourism, those programs that feature magical encounters with tortoises or moments sitting under a banyan tree and listening to the birds. While architectural tours that include sitting under an overpass and listening to the expressway roar seem to be a stretch, I have witnessed sound-and-light shows, like the one in Hong Kong, that turn contemporary works of architecture into theater. Media coverage of buildings like the Guggenheim Bilbao duly stress the resplendent wonder gained by the architectural visit. But do the hordes of tourists learn much about the city of Bilbao beyond the monument and its associated tourist infrastructure? Do they stay long enough to acquire a larger awareness of the outer neighborhoods of the city or the Basque region? Can mass tourism, drawn by the icon, subsequently be channeled into a larger engagement with the built environment and historical culture?

These questions frame some of the salient characteristics of mass tourism. In *The Tourist* (1976, 1989), Dean MacCannell comments on the autonomy of the tourist world and the way it is "constructed after the fashion of all worlds that are filled with people who are just passing through and know it."[4] No doubt, the perception of architecture changes dramatically when people leave their homes and take to the road. On the tourist trail, we are more sensitive to the sights around us. Familiar places and panoramas disappear. Routines—

whether in commute or on errand—are left behind. So too are the demands of daily life, work, family, and leisure. In unfamiliar territory, without proximate obligations or spatial orientation, it becomes much harder to look without looking. Groping in a new geography, we have to look much more closely. Our senses are thus freed to a remarkable extent. Potentially, the itinerary is wide open and adventures lurk around every corner. Ideally, the sheer weight of the unknown results in a full-blown sensory encounter with all aspects of the passing built environment. Travel of this sort starts to sound like the voyage of the Surrealists into the city as dreamscape, or the concept of the *dérive*, popularized by Guy Debord and the Situationists, a journey into changing urban ambiances and their new psychic atmospheres. It becomes not only an aesthetic pleasure but also an act of liberation.

While travel does resemble this description for some of us some of the time, an overwhelming density of the unknown can also shut down our senses. It is hard to revel in a streetscape at midnight when one is desperately trying to find a hotel with a vacancy. Likewise, it is not easy to exult in a strange building while anxiously awaiting a bus already hours late. For these reasons, many of us prefer to reduce the quantity of the unknown by booking advance transportation, lodging, and even sightseeing excursions. Mass tourism cushions the impact of arrival and enables the visitor to negotiate large and potentially confusing stretches of territory.

Advance historical and architectural preparations also deepen perception. Romantics might prefer to view the tourist trail as a never-ending series of absolutely original and unprepared-for experiences with built form and space. In actuality, the possibility of such an aesthetic depends on considerable erudition. Especially with unfamiliar buildings in unfamiliar places, the more we know the more we are drawn into the encounter. Tourists, historians, and architects alike appreciate having a fuller idea of what they will be seeing on their travels.

In mass tourism, therefore, a dose of familiarization is required if the unfamiliar is to hold its appeal. The problem lies in the extent to which familiarization can turn the unfamiliar into the all-too-recognizable. Must mass tourism, as many of us have experienced, resemble the mass media, a parade of hits driven by proven formulas? The hits have to change in order to whet our interest. The formulas must be modulated from time to time. Yet traveling between the monuments of the world can be as repetitive as channel surfing, and as isolating. When too many arrangements are made beforehand no room is left for spontaneity. Since most architectural monuments, including the contemporary ones, spawn a considerable surrounding infrastructure of shops, restaurants, hotels, and other amusements, free time is often concentrated in a separate tourist precinct. Only a fraction of tourists manage, sometimes by accident, to venture outside this zone into the neighborhoods of the city. The perception of the architectural monument occurs against a homogeneous backdrop rather than an environment of local diversity and uniqueness. Do people look as closely and freshly in such circumstances? Given the brevity of time and the quantity of stuff jammed into the tour, will the tourist's prejudices about different peoples and places be challenged? Given the vendors and crowds blanketing the sites, will the tourist even see much of a building?

A tourist couple looks at the Taj Mahal in Agra, India, 2004. Photo: Manish Swarup, AP Photo

Japanese tourists take pictures on wooden walkways in St. Mark's Square flooded by high water in Venice, 2001. Photo: Francesco Proietti

Over the past couple of decades these conditions have been exacerbated. Whereas it was once uncommon to shop for ordinary clothing items while on vacation, brand-name stores and outlet malls have popped up all over the world. One buys not only souvenirs outside the architectural monument but also personal and household items, the identical kinds of shorts or running shoes available back home. Similarly, with the spread of franchised restaurants and hotels, it is possible to eat and sleep in circumstances that are remarkably alike, and tune into CNN and HBO almost anywhere.

Quite incongruously, the architecture of a tourist precinct (and sometimes an entire city) often comes under the influence of its guiding historical style. To preserve or enhance a sense of place, local architects are encouraged to design new buildings and complexes that continue the look, say, of Santa Fe adobe or Bavarian Fachwerk or Jerusalem stone. Put simply, the tourist precinct themes itself. Tourists, often unaware of what's fact and what's *faux*, end up perceiving the architectural echoes of a monument in a host of vernacular buildings, including their chain hotel or restaurant. A staged representational field extends all around where once a wide variety of historical buildings stood. How will the urge to theme play out over the years in the realm of architourism? Will there be imitative reverberations of Gehry's titanium curves, or will the climate of the architecturally audacious allow for bold experimentation in any number of directions? Whatever happens, it seems clear that the future design of all tourist precincts will be calibrated to entice and hold as many eyes and wallets as possible.

In the end, it might be romantic to imagine that mass tourism in the twenty-first century can spark the sensations of strangeness that tourism did in past eras. With images of architecture readily available in a wide array of formats, first sightings of the famous

monuments have changed. The shock of the new is more or less replaced by the satisfaction of recognition. Mass tourism is indeed like mass media. The lure of the new works best when the new is both anticipated and well packaged. In 1925, in his essay "Travel and Dance," Siegfried Kracauer already remarked that tourists are prepared for foreign places through the perusal of illustrated magazines.[5] Nowadays, through coffee-table books, friends' JPEGs, television ads, and movie trailers, tourists are well prepped for their on-site architectural experiences. A profusion of tour guides, and especially Internet sites, launches the tourist into touring weeks or months before the actual trip begins. What is striking about this body of preparatory information is the degree to which issues of touring comfort and efficiency take precedence over historical information about architecture or place.

From the airport to the air-conditioned bus to the four- or five-star hotel, package tourists spend much of their time within a cocoon. They might as well be at home, or at the mall, or in a multiplex with stadium seating and surround sound. The orchestrated itineraries, with their chosen spots for lecturing, picture taking and shopping, and their frequent driving ellipses over ignorable terrain are similar to the experience of movies and television. The tour, like mass media, picks choice viewing angles, provides a steady stream of voice-overs, and is relentless in its efficient editing of built environments that are deemed unpleasant, unrewarding, or too complicated. In an age of fast cutting, in which images stay on the screen only fractions of a second, can we expect the tour to proceed slowly and randomly? Tourists rightly demand to be taken to the best spot at an optimum moment for a succinct amount of time. Mission accomplished. Time to speed to the next attraction.

What kind of architectural experience arises in such circumstances? By removing many of travel's unpredictable and unpleasant aspects, are mass tourists becoming floating bodies and eyes manipulated by the hands of company puppeteers? By focusing so much on the jewel of destination—or a necklace of destinations—does the wonder of journey get lost? It is easy to imagine people having fantastic, if brief, aesthetic encounters. But it is equally easy to predict eventual exhaustion. Like a visit to a world-class museum, its halls lined with masterpieces, seamless tourism through a succession of architectural monuments undoubtedly induces great fatigue and casual attentiveness. I have often noticed that the first couple of days of a trip are the most exhilarating. Each succeeding day the sights stand out less and less as exceptional sights. Mass tourism runs into the problem Sigmund Freud raised with regard to the pleasure principle. According to Freud, great joy can only be episodic, an upwelling of emotion that immediately follows frustration, boredom, or sadness: "When any situation that is desired by the pleasure principle is prolonged, it only produces a feeling of mild contentment. We are so made that we can derive intense enjoyment only from a contrast and very little from a state of things."[6] On the package tour, when the state of things becomes a routine of visits to architectural masterpieces, should it be surprising that tourists eventually come to dread lingering in yet another cathedral, temple, or museum? Evidently, there can be too much of a good thing.

But somehow the group tours keep on coming and going. Mass tourism is incredibly big business. Museums and other significant architectural works have never in history been so popular, and so enmeshed in the marketplace. Visitor and dollar counts as well as economic multiplier effects dominate media discussions of architourism. What does it mean that more than one million people journey to Bilbao each year to visit the Guggenheim? As I have argued in this essay, commodity economics condition the perception of architecture in tourist environments, weighted toward buildings that are priceless and contexts that are predictable and profitable. Architourism favors a streaming sort of perception, composed of pithy views, and their often simultaneous representations via the camera lens. As monuments are increasingly photographed and filmed, as tours more cleverly compose a tourist's viewing experience, architecture becomes a stage set for brief visual highs. Instead of offering time for leisurely reflection and close examination, which the tourist would be unable to handle day after day, the tour moves rapidly in and out. The building, glanced at quickly, takes on the emotional language of distance and remove, somewhat like the aura of a movie star—enhanced if the building is by a brand-name architect.

In the years to come, it would not be surprising to witness many more buildings sold as architourism and more modern masterpieces resurrected as sites of package pilgrimage. Many of these sites and works are located in older, industrial cities that have suffered since the onset of the service and information economy. Why would any of these cities not try to sell their potential built resources or develop new ones? Why wouldn't these cities want to cash in on the drawing power of a Gehry or a Calatrava or a reinvented Wright?

Will architourism stimulate the creation of lasting masterpieces? Possibly. Any situation that lavishes great amounts of money and attention on architecture can't be a bad thing. But it is doubtful that architectural monuments can be created on demand in record numbers. In the past, such works were rare achievements, crowning moments of a place and time. Older monuments derive lasting tourist value in large part because of the considerable profundity and duration of their respective cultures. The appeal of their architecture is directly linked to the fascination tourists have for the lore of their cultures—the gods and warriors, the emperors and concubines, the spies and revolutionaries. Form alone captivates architects to a much greater extent than the mass public or tourist. Alas, architourism's appeal is largely formal. Its works are driven by our age's captivation with theatrical spectacle. One wonders, given contemporary culture's fickleness and impatience, how long this spectacle will appear fresh and compelling. What will happen when the marketplace moves on to something else, as it always does?

Isn't it likely that the parade of architourism will suffer the fate of all things new? Unlike the everlasting appeal of great age, novelty wears off quickly. Or does architourism promise an architectural semblance of eternal youth? Like museums and older monuments, contemporary works are entombed within the stasis peculiar to the tourist precinct. They are viewed amid tourism's exclusion of most other political, cultural, and even economic forces. The contemporary building is therefore timeless from its inception, canonized

before it is realized, an object of scholarship and preservation before its outer skin has had the time to take on a patina of soot and stains. Through architourism, tourists encounter the new stopped dead in its tracks.

Likewise, through architourism, tourists encounter buildings connected far more to timeless celebrity than to historical geography. Given their current global proliferation, why will people travel to Bilbao in the future if they can see a Gehry in Los Angeles or closer to home? Indeed, it is fair to say that the new architourist monuments are really non-places.[7] They are pieces on a global assembly line, relating as much to their location as do the brand-name products and franchised businesses that surround them. They resemble the new airports and hotels that frame a visit more than do the traditional monuments seen on the same trip. Unlike those older buildings, these contemporary buildings are created with a fleeting tourist sensibility in mind; their site is most of all a passage on an endless train of sights. The meaning of such a tourist architecture can only be gleaned within this larger chain of transit: an image spread in a tourist brochure; the journey on an airplane, bus, or other vehicle; a hotel; dinner somewhere; the immersion with cameras and postcards at the site and afterward; the hotel pool; the purchase and display of souvenirs; and other visits to architectural monuments. The work of architourism, while gazed at in aesthetic rapture on-site, calls into existence a far larger range of states of consciousness—distraction, anticipation, expectation, exhaustion, diversion, possession, relief, recollection—that occur before, during, and after the trip. The work of architourism, while it benefits its region economically, extends its reach across the globe.

In light of all these matters, will architourism lead the mass public to develop a substantially deeper understanding of architecture? Likely not. Its perception of buildings, like most other things, will be brief and fragmentary, part and parcel of a larger mediated viewing experience. And is that so bad? Architourism puts at least a thick slice of architecture out there on the public's plate. It encourages tourists to seek out new views, not only in the remote past but also in the here and now. It provides a city or region with a glorious new building that can help to energize architectural culture. Most of all, it lends a role for the sensuality of building in a time of artificial intelligences and representations. Against the array of mediated and digitized encounters proliferating in the marketplace—from plasma screens to iPods—architourism might just be the architectural discipline's best shot at a contemporary hit machine.

NOTES

1. Lucy Lippard, *On the Beaten Track: Tourism, Art, and Place* (New York: The New Press, 1999), 164.

2. John Urry, *The Tourist Gaze: Leisure and Travel in Contemporary Societies* (London: Sage Publications, 1990), 139.

3. Briavel Holcomb, "Marketing Cities for Tourism," in *The Tourist City*, edited by Dennis R. Judd and Susan S. Fainstein (New Haven: Yale University Press, 1999), 54.

4. Dean MacCannell, *The Tourist: A New Theory of the Leisure Class*, rev. 2d ed. (New York: Schocken Books, 1989), 51.

5. Siegfried Kracauer, *The Mass Ornament: Weimar Essays*, translated by Thomas Y. Levin (Cambridge, Mass.: Harvard University Press, 1995), 66.

6. Sigmund Freud, *Civilization and Its Discontents* [1930], translated by James Strachey (New York: W.W. Norton, 1961), 25.

7. Marc Augé, *Non-Places: Introduction to an Anthropology of Supermodernity*, translated by John Howe (London: Verso, 1995), 78–79.

NINE SITE-SEERS

Installation view of *Architourism: Architecture as a Destination for Tou*
Arthur Ross Gallery, Columbia University, 2002. Photo: Eduard Hueber

Motivated by a desire for authentic experience or for exotic places, for escape or spectacle, or simply by an urge for new knowledge, the tourist leaves a familiar environment to view other locations through the lens of his or her own memories, expectations, and fantasies. And whether received in a mode of distraction or attention, perceived as background or foreground, architecture has always been an integral part of the tourist's experience. Today, as places increasingly get restructured as spaces of consumption, and as tourist activities merge with other mass-consumption practices, from shopping and sports to culture and education, architecture is becoming an integral part of the conception and economy of tourism, and vice versa. The nine projects that appear on yellow pages throughout this book, by artists as well as architects, are not so much about how architects are designing buildings for tourism today as reflections on the ways in which, in an advanced consumer society, architecture constructs tourist experiences and is in turn constructed by tourist values.

Two projects relate to the contemporary airport. Diller + Scofidio's *Travelogues*, which appears on the following three pages as well as on the front and back cover, is a public artwork that confronts arriving passengers at JFK International Airport with a series of lenticular images that tell stories about travelers as revealed through the screening of their luggage at security checkpoints. Martha Rosler's *Airport Series* likewise addresses the effects of the airport system on the contemporary traveler's psyche. The strategy of standardized diversity—familiarity inflected with local variations or special effects—multiplies the banal spaces of this controlled and homogenized architectural environment where local differences don't make much difference. Not surprisingly, some surreality at times creeps into the anaesthetizing framework of sameness.

Tseng Kwong Chi's self-portraits with architectural monuments, from his *East Meets West* series, focus sharply on the relationship between identity and deterritorialization. Projecting himself as subject into his own images, the photographer literally embodies the alienation of the tourist gaze and while parodying the tourist's global-imperial ambitions. In a different vein, Mark Robbins's *Import / Export* juxtaposes Miami's tourist skyline with portraits of some of the city's newer immigrant workers. Originally presented as a series of billboards, the project advertises the disparity between tourist myths and the invisible economy that underwrites them.

Julian Rosefeldt and Piero Steinle also evoke contradictions between tourist space and "real" space in their respective still and video images of ambiances created for mass tourism and leisure. In two different escapist settings—the ephemeral Oktoberfest beer tents of Munich and the sublimely artificial landscapes of Iceland's public swimming pools—bacchanalian and pastoral dreams are pleasurably indulged.

Two other video projects, one by Anette Baldauf and Dorit Margreiter, the other by Silvia Kolbowski, explore the blurring of boundaries between high and low culture in the context of Las Vegas. In Kolbowski's loop of images and design slogans, *Something for Nothing,* the gambler's paradise becomes not so much an escape as inescapable, while high-end architecture seems, like dice, to be an obsessive pursuit for design-conscious consumers. In *Remake Las Vegas,* Baldauf and Margreiter pointedly reveal how, in a post-Venturian phase of development in that city, entertainment and art are increasingly indistinguishable programs from the standpoint of marketing and design.

Finally, Hans Haacke's die-cut poster, *Untitled (World Trade Center),* exposes, with an eloquently minimal gesture, the endless play of meanings opened up by the voids of the two towers in the collective consciousness of city, while at the same time anticipating the way the architectural afterimage becomes embedded in the circuits of advertising, popular culture, and everyday life.

JOAN OCKMAN

DILLER + SCOFIDIO
TRAVELOGUES

2002
38 lenticular screens, 4 x 4 feet each

This permanent public artwork in the new
International Arrivals Terminal 4 at New
York City's John F. Kennedy Airport
comprises a sequence of lenticular
screens. A lenticular screen is a lens in
sheet form that can produce an image with
depth and motion. As the eye moves
across the surface, the lens focuses it on
layered images beneath, producing a
sense of three-dimensionality and
animation. The installation exploits the
unidirectional movement of travelers
walking down a narrow corridor from
arrival gate to customs by creating a
series of one-second "films," similar to a
flipbook. The coherent mini-stories related
by these images, taken from film clips,
large-format transparencies, and medical
X rays, form a larger narrative about
people's travels related to the experience
of having their luggage screened at
security checkpoints. Viewed in its
entirety, *Travelogues* tells the tales of four
travelers. Passersby are transformed from
passive viewers into active interpreters of
a moving-picture narrative that provides
only bits of information—sometimes
nostalgic, sometimes surprising, humorous,
or mysterious.

AUTHENTIC

Authenticity is a slippery concept, and relatively unique in the philosophical lexicon in that it cannot be defined without also defining the inauthentic. That which is thought to be purposeful and real always stands in relationship to an antinomic Other. The origins of this can be traced back to the Enlightenment ambition to elevate consciousness above the obfuscations of myth and irrationality. The texts of Immanuel Kant, for example, are inhabited, if one reads them carefully, by the ghostly presences of various "dogmatists," "simpletons" and "shallow-pates," as Kant calls them, who, in one way or another, are incapable of participating in the shared goal of cultural advancement. They are not threats from outside the system, but rather are insiders whose presence constitutes a paradox in the Enlightenment project. Made visible by the light of Reason, they are at the same time defined as impervious to the potency of its claims.

From the early nineteenth century on, among those who have been slotted into the rung of inauthenticity, historians in particular must be mentioned. For this we largely can thank the philosopher Georg Wilhelm Friedrich Hegel. In his *Vorlesungen über die Philosophie der Geschichte* [Lectures on the Philosophy of History] (1821), he castigated those historians who, under the pretext of "higher criticism," introduced "all the antihistorical monstrosities that a vain imagination could suggest." In other words, in order for History (with a capital H) to be an autonomous and authentic expression of the philosophy of the mind, it had to be elevated above the contaminating—and contaminated—efforts of professional historians. Today's historians, especially in the field of art and architectural history, despite the success in establishing the norms of their discipline, still work within a space scarred by the dialectics of the Enlightenment's anti-historiographic philosophy. In Manfredo Tafuri and Francesco Dal Co's book *Modern Architecture* (1986), for instance, not a single historian is mentioned as having anything to do with the making or framing of the modernist aesthetic. Sigfried Giedion is referred to once, but is labeled, tellingly, as "a critic."

How the Enlightenment trope of authenticity came to be intertwined with the theorizing of modernism is, of course, a complex story, but an important factor was the emergence of psychology in the late nineteenth century. It gave scientific and disciplinary armature to the socio-philosophical premises of authenticity that had been developed in the nineteenth century. It was no accident that Friedrich Nietzsche called himself the first psychologist. It was no accident that Heinrich Wölfflin, who wrote his dissertation on the psychology of architecture, saw his book *Principles of Art History* (1915) not as a contribution to art history, but as defining the parameters of what he hoped would be a new discipline, namely, "Formpsychology."

It was no accident that someone like William Curtis, in writing recently about Le Corbusier, makes clear to his readers that he visited the sites about which he writes, adding, "I hitchhiked to see the real thing for myself." Finally, bringing the trope up to date, it is no accident that Arthur Danto, in critiquing an art history that, according to him, has "become pallidly academic…curatorialized, or worse, docentized," says to the visitors of an exhibition of Vermeer paintings: "Plant yourself in front of each painting…until you have gone as far in its tense aesthetic as you are able. You should exit in the exultant bafflement that is the mark of having experienced Vermeer truly."

The history of the authenticity/inauthenticity trope (if one includes in the discussion all its various subtexts, whether they are covertly or overtly applied) is key in the formulation of a critical history of the Enlightenment-modernist project. It touches not only on the history of the different sciences and philosophies of the Self but also on such obviously related phenomena as the history of capitalism, politics, and tourism. This is not to say that authenticity is relative; very much to the contrary. It is bound up in a network of reinforcing and referential systems, the historical end of which has not yet arrived, given the lure to continually leverage "authenticity" for one purpose or another.

It is not without some irony that today the once much-maligned medium of history can now see authenticity for the social and cultural construction that it is. And therein, of course, lies the rub. If modernism could still proclaim the authenticity of history (or, perhaps better stated, the authenticity of its history), namely, one in which historians could only be outsiders and thus invisible to its advances, today there is at least balance to the equation. The philosophical project lies now with historians just as much with artists, whose common mission, so I hold, is no longer to provide the groundwork of the substantiation of Being, but to bring out of hiding Enlightenment's productive unclarities.

What this shows in a small way is that the old Enlightenment hope of directing our civilizational ambitions by differentiating between the authentic and the inauthentic is simply no longer sufficient for the understanding of the very modernity that this distinction once entailed. In fact, once we sever the link between authenticity and modernity, and challenge the flip side of that equation, namely, between history and authenticity, we face the need for a more fluid, critical perspective that can prove that we as citizens and as scholars are more than capable of living outside these ideological controls.

MARK JARZOMBEK

CHRISTIANE HERTEL
BEYOND IN/AUTHENTICITY: DRESDEN'S FRAUENKIRCHE

Since the 1960s, critical perspectives on the concept of authenticity have ranged from Theodor W. Adorno's *Jargon of Authenticity* (1966), his relentless polemic against what he considered a deceptive version of Heideggerian ontology, to Richard Shiff's elucidation of modern and postmodern notions of artistic authenticity in his essay "Original Copy" (1994).[1] Within this range, the dialectical critique according to which that which is postulated as authentic turns out to be inauthentic. This dialectic implies another notion of authenticity, one that would seem to reside in what Jürgen Habermas, writing in 1980, midway between the above-mentioned texts, called the "incomplete project of modernity"—that is, of enlightenment.[2] Yet Max Horkheimer and Adorno's *Dialectic of Enlightenment* (1947) had clearly demonstrated this project's limitations, which are posed by the inability of free thinking to comprehend and control nature within and without humanity, and which grow in direct proportion to the ever increasing technological control of nature.

Shiff lays out a similar problem in his discussion of contemporary artist Vija Celmins's *To Fix the Image in Memory* (1977–82), which pairs eleven geologically different rocks found in northern New Mexico with their painted bronze copies.[3] This is not to suggest, however, that Celmins's project shared Adorno's cultural pessimism. On the contrary, it may be argued that her challenge to the viewer's ability to compare and distinguish nature and art opened the possibility of a productive, if disconcerting, poetic liberation of memory from the need to assert authenticity or its opposite.

Thus, the problem of authenticity seems to extend beyond the grasp of an insightful dialectical critique of in/authenticity, and this becomes self-evident in the field of historic preservation, where the pairing of stones is at stake, yet where the stones have a human history, where individual memory is aligned with a purported objective and collective memory, and where nevertheless the range of judgments in a given case may turn out to be neither entirely hierarchical nor fully democratic, but instead kaleidoscopic. Even so, most of these judgments are eventually committed to private and public archives

and to public oblivion. This happens because of practical issues—the inevitability of final decision-making and its physical consequences, which seem to assert themselves as built truth. Furthermore, historic preservation cannot help but edit each case's historical specificity and its particular reception and perception. Such an editorial process, especially if pursued with the goal of returning to an original authenticity preceding a monument's "afterlife," might involve a considerable difference between what one feels to be authentic and what, on the basis of archaeological research, one knows to be authentic.

In the specific context of historic preservation in Germany, questions of authenticity seem inseparable from questions of identity and historical responsibility. Speaking as a scholar, I tend to rationalize my own experience and emotions as a tourist, thus making them an ultimately immeasurable part of my discourse. In view of what I have sketched out above, I see this as a legitimate dialectical process, and yet I remain acutely aware of the taboo attached to fully addressing the gap between what we can know and what we feel.[4] In part, this taboo arises from a sense of propriety that shuns an unseemly narcissism in scholarly discourse. But it is also the result of an inconvenience, the inconvenience of a destabilizing

factor in scholarship that merits some reflection. I can illustrate this with the example of my research on the current reconstruction of the Frauenkirche in Dresden, which has led me to a critique of what I see as an at best misguided and at worst purposely deceptive appropriation of the project on the part of the political and economic establishment during the later years of the Helmut Kohl era, beginning with the reunification of Germany in 1990.

The municipal Lutheran Frauenkirche designed by Georg Bähr (1726–43) was once one of Dresden's most famous landmarks. After the city's destruction in February 1945, it was preserved as a ruin and eventually, in 1967, declared a memorial to the civilian victims of the bombing. How complicated the Frauenkirche's double status as ruin and monument was became clear early in the process of its "archaeological reconstruction," undertaken since 1990. Central to the vigorous public debate in 1990–91 was the issue of whether this reconstruction entailed the obliteration of historical consciousness and of a local collective memory.

The possibility that a monument's preservation might actually mean its death has been debated by theorists of historic preservation ever since Alois Riegl published his essay "The Modern Cult of Monuments"

Aerial view of Neumarkt with the Frauenkirche, Dresden, Germany, 1926. Photo: Walter Hahn. Sächsische Landesbibliothek, Deutsche Fotothek

in 1903.[5] The destruction of cities in World War II framed this question in new ways unforeseen by Riegl.[6] In the case of the Frauenkirche it is clear that the building long ago lost its originally intended meaning(s) to others no less believed to inhere in it. While accepting the coexistence of multiple meanings, however, the particular practice of "archaeological reconstruction" aims to regain the Frauenkirche's general or summary landmark character and thereby weakens its specific function as a war memorial. The context of this shift is primarily political. In this context, namely, of German reunification, the reconstruction of the Frauenkirche has come to represent a very specific gesture of historical founding.

Such a use of the church was not new. When in May 1967, on the occasion of the national Arbeitertestspiele (Workers' Festival) in Dresden, the ruin was publicly declared a memorial to the civilian victims of the bombing and thus, by allegorical extension, also a memorial to its own ruination in 1945, this rededication of the Frauenkirche additionally declared the end of the "Trümmerzeit," the postwar era of rubble and ruin.[7] Especially in West Germany, the memorial ruin was a welcome and seemingly unalterable given, whereas in Dresden the hope for the reconstruction of the Frauenkirche never entirely perished. Therefore it is not surprising that the idea of undertaking this project was voiced immediately after the fall of the Berlin Wall.

Fritz Löffler, Dresden's outspoken advocate for art, architecture, and historic preservation in East Germany, already used the term "archaeological reconstruction" in his standard work, *Das alte Dresden* (1955).[8] The private foundation entrusted in 1990 with the reconstruction understood it to mean both the archaeological excavation of the site and, aided by computer technology, the authentic reuse of original building materials as well as the reincorporation of the intact foundations and remnants of walls that had remained standing for forty-five years.[9] The reconstruction logo visualizes this rebuilt whole Frauenkirche, as does a Lego-block model—one of the more ingenious fund-raising efforts to be conceived, which allowed the general public to play at reconstruction by joining, for a fee, black and white blocks until the model was completed.

The incorporation of reusable material, the structurally sound practice of eighteenth-century building techniques, the application of historic craftsmanship to the supplemental new blocks quarried from the same or similar sites as the old ones—all of this was intended to recreate faithfully the eighteenth-century Frauenkirche with the utmost degree of material truth and conceptual authenticity. It would, according to the belief of Heinrich Magirius, State Conservator of Saxony, return Dresden to the power of persuasion and truthfulness manifest in what he called its original architect's *Bekenntnis,* which may be translated as "conviction" or even "creed" in stone.[10] Gerhard Glaser, head of the Institute for Historic Preservation in Dresden, argued similarly that "this reconstruction must do justice to the inner truth of the building and must contain as much of the original substance in the rebuilt Frauenkirche as possible—as a matter of principle, but also in order to preserve remembrance of the past in the reconstructed building of hope."[11] According to these two statements, dating from as late as 1994 and 1995, the reconstructed Frauenkirche was decidedly not intended to be a replica of a lost building. Its truth and authenticity, however, would owe themselves to current computer technology, which during the excavation helped locate each major building block's original place on the facade. Such technology, perhaps, was thought not only to make possible but also, precisely by virtue of its scientific objectivity, to partake in such truthfulness.

As soon as these plans for "archaeological reconstruction" were formulated in 1990, they stirred an extended public debate in Dresden and across Germany, in architectural periodicals, magazines, daily newspapers, and in symposia, both local and national.[12] One very important question raised was whether this reconstruction did not effectively obliterate the status of the Frauenkirche as a signifier of German "historical consciousness." At the time, this phrase had several associations, including that of Nazi Germany, of

Dresden's destruction in 1945, of the forty years of the East German state and society, and of the claim of the East German opposition and peace movement of the 1980s to this particular ruin and memorial as a symbol of hope and reform. The site was excavated between January 1993 and May 1994, and since then the building has gone up and been finished ahead of the intended deadline, 2006, the eight-hundredth anniversary of the city. In 1994, at the time of the excavation's completion and the reconstruction's groundbreaking ceremony, a financial crisis was revealed, necessitating a reconstitution of the Frauenkirche Foundation in charge of the project and its rescue and underwriting by the Dresdner Bank. What had started in November 1989 as an initiative of local citizens became, from this point on, a project of the political center right, that is, of an alliance of political and financial power, with the Evangelical Lutheran Church of Saxony in the position of being one of three cofounders (along with the city of Dresden and the state of Saxony) and Saxony's Institute of Historic Preservation now primarily in an advisory role.[13] Meanwhile, the original Society for the Reconstruction of the Frauenkirche has continued its efforts at private fundraising. Other organizations, both private and public, local, national, and international, including the American "Friends of Dresden" and the Dresdner Bank itself, have raised funds as well.

One of the changes resulting from the foundation's reconfiguration was the loosening of the initially rigorously pursued goal of "historical," or "material," truth. For example, in addition to using original building material supplemented by newly quarried sandstone, it was decided in February 1996 to use blocks salvaged from the eighteenth-century bridge in Torgau, which had recently been exploded to make room for a new bridge.[14] Even so, all proposals to include a critically reflective "alienation effect" (*Verfremdungseffekt*), to borrow Brecht's term, some of which actually postdate the 1994 reconfiguration, were ruled out, with the exception of Anish Kapoor's sculpture, or altar, in the center of the former burial vaults, which were rebaptized the "Lower Church." Kapoor's altar is part of a proposal to give these vaults over to several other internationally well-known artists for thematic installations. In addition to Kapoor, Ilya Kabakov, Moshe Gershuni, Marina Abramovic, and Magdalena Jetlová were initially invited to participate.

Other proposals, taking as their model Egon Eiermann's Kaiser Wilhelm-Gedächtniskirche in Berlin, suggested an entirely new building sharply juxtaposed with the ruin, or else at least the encasing of one of the ruined church entrances in glass. Hans Nadler, Dresden's highly respected second postwar conservator, suggested leaving one very large fragment of cornice on the ground next to the church.[15] In that case, something comparable to Vija Celmins's *To Fix the Image in Memory* would have been achieved, for the fallen piece of cornice would have been paired with its copy incorporated into the building. This might have pointed up the complexity of the project and acknowledged its new "material truth."

It is important to realize that the particular concern raised about this project in the early 1990s, namely, that the Frauenkirche's reconstruction might fail to preserve the ruin's functions as memorial, was

The Frauenkirche ruin as seen from a terrace, Thonig, Dresden, Germany, 1966. Sächsische Landesbibliothek, Deutsche Fotothek

not solely grounded in historical piety, but advanced in the context of considerable East and West German disillusionment with the process of reunification and also with some of its results. In this context the Frauenkirche's emerging appearance could suggest the political allegory of a victory monument. Such a bitter reading would seem to vindicate one of the project's outspoken opponents on the West German Left, Reinhard Bentmann, an architectural historian and state conservator in Wiesbaden, Hessen, who predicted in 1993 that once completed, the Frauenkirche would stand above all as proof of a counterfeit German history and would mark the 1990s as a decade utterly lacking in a vision for the future. But however trenchant Bentmann's view remains, his alternative proposal, namely, to allow for the Frauenkirche's decay or "fall in dignity" (*Untergang in Würde*), was itself quite problematic, precisely because it gave over the power of decision-making to nature.[16]

On the other hand, what has come to pass instead is the calculated naturalization of a political process. The Kohl era turned the Frauenkirche into a monument to Germany's unification. What was unified politically, East and West Germany, would become unified symbolically in joining the excavated foundations and building materials to the necessary new masonry, and to Western technological and financial know-how. The East came to stand for both the temporary and the old, whereas the West came to stand for both the new and yet also what endures and is alone legitimate. The allegedly natural, or objective, character of the process was achieved and visualized through the careful conjunction of "old"—dark and sooted—with "new"— bright and clean ashlar blocks—which eventually, after some weathering and air pollution, will all come to look the same. In terms of geological age and process, this sameness is a given.[17] However, for as long as it will be visually evident, this decision on building materials for the Frauenkirche's facade reflects a notable change in ideological color coding. Whereas prior to 1989 red stood for the East and black for the West, in the reunified Germany as represented by the reconstructed Frauenkirche, dark/black denoted the East, bright/white the West, and red disappeared. In this way, according to the mission statement in both German and English on a construction site billboard, the reconstruction would return the church, and by implication, the East, to "the world of culture" (the West), as if rescuing it from an uncivilized state of existence. As the above account demonstrates, however, the monument's purported rescue from nature actually amounts to the naturalization of a political present under the guise of a scientifically accurate preservation of national heritage.

So far I have laid out my critical and largely dialectical understanding of the reconstruction of the Frauenkirche and the functions of the concept of authenticity in the project. I now return to some "inconvenient" aspects of this project and also of its critique, which raise the possibility that the most powerful claim to authenticity is local experience. Whether their object is exploited, corrupted, commodified, rejected, or criticized, local claims to authenticity, even as they differ and compete, demand respect by virtue of being based in local knowledge and experience. While such respect may and should entail a dilemma for those making decisions about historic preservation such as the ones described here, they also play a role in the work of the scholarly observer. Two examples of personal encounters with local answers to the question of the Frauenkirche's authenticity may serve to illustrate this point.

Since 1992, and at least until November 2002, every Saturday, rain or shine, a retired physicist has offered hourly tours of the Frauenkirche, first of the excavation site and then of the building rising from the original foundations. In the mid–1990s, I joined his tours a few times. Afterward I spoke to him about the various criticisms of the reconstruction and the fact that tourists may be conditioned, for example, by an advertisement posted nationwide by the Dresdner Bank urging the sponsorship of new ashlar blocks as the equivalent to donating, literally, "a piece of German history." He was aware of these issues, but this did not shake his belief in the initial civic spirit of the reconstruction, which he seemed to hope would quietly persist. Guiding

thousands of tourists through this ever-changing site, he was able to perceive or present it as true to this spirit, whose authenticity for him apparently transcended the project's considerably changed political framework as well as the touristic curiosity about it. In the fall of 2002, the Frauenkirche Web site still listed his tours and he was pictured on it, preferring, as he has throughout the years, to remain anonymous. His strategy is, in a way, both simpler and more radical than that of the establishment I have criticized, or even my own critique. It strikes me as an East German kind of Kantian ethic, which subjectively naturalizes and thereby disempowers the powers-that-be as of only seasonal and mechanical importance. It views their self-interest as in the end serving but not corrupting a cause considered to be a common good, namely, *Kulturerbe,* cultural heritage and its inherent civilizing power.[18] Here authenticity is a matter of enduring belief and felt duty. In relation to the authors mentioned at the beginning of my essay, this tour guide implicitly sided with Habermas against Horkheimer and Adorno.

My second example involves betrayed loyalty. When in Dresden in the 1990s, I stayed with a family who for several generations had lived in one of the city's suburbs and had been able to hold onto its private property under the pressures of East German socialism. In the 1970s the husband and wife commissioned a student at the Munich Art Academy to copy the photographic reproduction they sent to him of a detail from Bernardo Bellotto's 1749–51 painting of the Frauenkirche and the Neumarkt in Dresden. The artist's painting hangs in the Dresden Painting Gallery of old masters, and yet this couple felt the need to own and display a piece of Bellotto's celebratory rendering of the church in their living room. This, indeed, is one version of Richard Shiff's "original copy," which by virtue of its visually immeasurable difference from its model evokes and perhaps even represents an imaginary original. The imaginary original, then, is not the Bellotto painting; it is the lost church. In an implicit act of personal and political resistance to the ruin's official function in socialist East Germany and through multilayered means of reproduction, this couple had

Frauenkirche reconstruction, combining "old" and "new" blocks, Dresden, Germany, 1996. Photo: Christiane Hertel

mourned the Frauenkirche as a landmark and a work of aesthetic merit that had been authenticated as such by an eighteenth-century Italian court painter in Dresden. The German word for landmark, *Wahrzeichen,* means a distinctive sign enabling one to recognize, to verify, and to remember a place by means of a monument, often a building or statue unique to it. In short, a landmark/ *Wahrzeichen* authenticates a place and its memory.[19] Yet, like many people I talked to, this couple thought of Dresden as doubly victimized, by both the Western Allies and the Soviet Union, and therefore they hypostatized the pre–1945 landmark as pure and uncorrupted. Initially, they fell into the reconstruction project's ideological trap. In 1990 and for several more years, they were excited about the reconstruction, which they experienced as "truly elevating."

Like tourists from elsewhere and yet also feeling a sense of local entitlement, they visited the site regularly, bought the "Frauenkirche watch" containing a splinter of stone from the church—one of the first items in an ever-growing selection of fundraising merchandise—and took pride in the project. But gradually their excitement was dampened by what they felt was the pushy West German takeover of Dresden and the East. They felt so disappointed by German unification and alienated from their city that they no longer went downtown. Forty years of East German socialism did not succeed in what seven or eight years of unified Germany managed to accomplish, namely,

Dresden Neumarkt with Frauenkirche by Bernardo
Bellotto, 1749–51, Staatliche Kunstsammlungen Dresden,
Germany, Germäldegalerie Alte Meister. Photo: Jürgen
Karpinski, Verlag Brück & Sohn

giving this couple a deeply felt experience of
alienation, even expropriation, and, in this sense, of
the new Frauenkirche's inauthenticity. They probably
still have their painting on the wall, a newly
configured, personal sign of resistance or defiance.

Both these examples are anecdotal and easily could
be dismissed as such. Yet I acknowledge that the
individuals described have influenced my scholarship in
some way. What I have to conclude, then, is that I
cannot determine the point at which art or architectural
history ends and "architourism" begins. Moreover, while
looking and listening sometimes amount to
authenticating, the distinction between looking and
listening, on the one hand, and authenticating, on the
other, is predicated on retrospective judgment, a
judgment that is probably revised more than once. This
much I know from my own evolving response to the
Frauenkirche, where at first looking and listening were
anything but critical and instead part of an experience
entirely based in an aesthetics of experience
(*Erlebnisaesthetik*).[20]

As a West German, I first came to Dresden in 1990
not to study the Frauenkirche but to undertake research
in the State Art Collection's department of works on
paper. It was my first visit to the former German East. I
marveled at the magical beauty of the Dresden Zwinger,
and was shaken by the sight of the looming war ruins in
the city's historic center, something I had not expected
to find there anymore, and was especially moved by the
ruin of the Frauenkirche, which I had expected to see. I
read the following inscription (in German, of course) on
a bronze plaque set directly into the ground next to the
statue of Martin Luther in front of it: "The Frauenkirche
in Dresden/ destroyed in February 1945 by Anglo-
American bombers/ built by Georg Bähr/ 1726–1743/
Its ruin commemorates the tens of thousands of dead
and admonishes the living to fight against imperialistic
barbarism and for peace and the happiness of
mankind." At that moment I did not question the
adequacy of this text to the ruin's symbolic meaning,
and I was shocked by the news of the reconstruction
project. "But they cannot do this," I thought in
disbelief, "They cannot do away with the memorial!" In
short, I was the ideal, if belated, tourist to Dresden in its
former East German identity: I knew next to nothing
about the city's postwar history, was moved to tears by
both its ruin and the ruin's beauty, and simply
authenticated what I saw. Soon, however, the critical
art historian in me realized that the dedication plaque
next to the church ruin was a prime example of Cold
War rhetoric, and "imperialistic barbarism" referred to
the Western Allies of World War II, NATO, and a
remilitarized West Germany alike. In the 1960s the
local architectural conservators had colluded with this
use of the Frauenkirche ruin, in part because it saved
the heap of stones from being used as a quarry and
subsequently bulldozed, and thus from the fate of other
ruins of historic buildings in this period.

While as a scholar I remain convinced that the
finished Frauenkirche will be powerfully inauthentic,
even uncanny, I can only speculate on what my initial
response to it will be when I visit it for the first time.
The attention I have paid here to the inconvenient
aspects of a critique of the Frauenkirche's

reconstruction demonstrates a close relation between the problems of in/authenticity and ideology—here, mainly political ideology—and between both of these and personal experience. There is yet another aspect to all this: I still marvel at the Zwinger's aesthetic qualities, even though, or perhaps because, I have studied its postwar history. From this I must conclude that the rigorous historical and critical account of in/authenticity does not fully account for its grip. On the contrary, just as the Zwinger's immediate postwar reconstruction history is now known to very few of its users, visitors, and admirers, so undoubtedly the Frauenkirche's immediate post-reunification reconstruction history will be obscure to most. That this is so is part of Dresden's local knowledge too, which is why the aesthetic and architectural merit of the Frauenkirche and its future use have figured so prominently in the language employed there by those promoting the project. What may well be forgotten is the problematic human agency in this naturalization of history and, with it, the question of in/authenticity.

NOTES

1. Richard Shiff, "Original Copy," *Common Knowledge* 3:1 (1994), 88–107.

2. Jürgen Habermas, "Modernity—An Incomplete Project," in Hal Foster, ed., *The Anti-Aesthetic: Essays on Postmodern Culture* (Port Townsend, Wash.: Bay Press, 1983), 3–15. On the limitations of Habermas's position see Gianni Vattimo, "The End of Modernity, the End of the Project," and "Ornament/Monument," in Neil Leach, ed., *Rethinking Architecture: A Reader in Cultural Theory* (London: Routledge, 1997), 148–60.

3. Shiff, "Original Copy," 93–95. On Celmins's project, see Judith Tannenbaum, *Vija Celmins*, with essays by Douglas Blau and Dave Hickey (Philadelphia: Institute for Contemporary Art, 1992), and Leo Costello, *Vija Celmins: Works from the Edward R. Broida Collection* (Houston: Museum of Fine Arts, 2002). I thank Leo Costello for discussing this piece with me.

4. A rare and brief attempt to address this gap is Eva Maria Höhle, "Das Gefühl in der Denkmalpflege," *Die Denkmalpflege* 52:2 (1994), 128–32.

5. Alois Riegl, "The Modern Cult of Monuments," translated by Kurt Forster, *Oppositions* 25 (1980), 21–51.

6. See, for example, two collections of essays, Wilfried Lipp, ed., *Denkmal—Werte—Gesellschaft: Zur Pluralität des Denkmalbegriffs* (Frankfurt: Campus, 1993), and Michael Diers, ed., *Mo(nu)mente: Formen und Funktionen ephemerer Denkmäler* (Berlin: Akademie Verlag, 1993).

7. Discussion and correspondence dating from May 1966 through March 1967 are documented in the Institut für Denkmalpflege Sachsen, *Arbeitsstelle Dresden* (hereafter referred to as IDS), DN, folder 1965–1974. Isolated inquiries from citizens suggest that the ruin's official dedication was something easily missed; they also testify to its popular meaning as a memorial prior to the dedication.

8. Fritz Löffler, *Das alte Dresden* (Frankfurt: Weidlich, 1966), 415: "archäologische Wiederherstellung vorbereitet."

9. See "Die Dresdner Frauenkirche: Geschichte—Zerstörung—Rekonstruktion," in *Dresdner Hefte* 32:4 (1992), passim, and

Ludwig Güttler et al., *Der Wiederaufbau der Frauenkirche zu Dresden, Eine Aufgabe von nationaler und internationaler Bedeutung: Aufruf zur Mithilfe* (Dresden: self-published, 1994).

10. Heinrich Magirius, "Der archäologische Wiederaufbau der Dresdner Frauenkirche: Eine wissenschaftstheoretische Grundlegung," in *Die Dresdner Frauenkirche: Jahrbuch zu ihrer Geschichte und zu ihrem archäologischen Wiederaufbau 1* (1995), 81–84, phrase quoted, 81. On the actual process of archaeological reconstruction, see Wolfram Jäger, "Bericht über die archäologische Enttrümmerung," ibid., 11–64; Eberhard Burger, "Erster Baubericht über den Wiederaufbau der Frauenkirche zu Dresden vom Januar 1993 bis Dezember 1994," ibid., 65–80; and the continuing discussion in the subsequent yearbooks. Some of this material is available in English in Wolfram Jäger and C. A. Brebbia, eds., *The Revival of Dresden* (Southhampton, UK: WIT Press, 2000).

11. IDS, DN Frauenkirche II, 1994– , position paper of October 10, 1994, 2 and 3. This and all other translations of sources in German are mine.

12. A comprehensive account of this controversy exceeds the framework of this article. Some of the most influential and also still accessible sources include, on the "pro" side, Jürgen Paul, "Eine Wiedergutmachung an Dresden," *Frankfurter Allgemeine Zeitung*, no. 290, December 13, 1990; Curt Siegel, "Und man braucht sie doch," *Die Zeit*, no. 7, February 8, 1991; and on the "contra" side, Manfred Sack, "Sterben und sterben lassen: Über den Umgang mit Ruinen und mit dem Verfall," *Die Zeit*, no. 33, August 10, 1990; and Ulrich Boehme, *Dona nobis pacem...* (Dresden: self-published, January 1991), on the ruin as "Symbol für Zusammenbruch in jeder Hinsicht."

13. For the foundation's new mission statement and rules and for membership on the boards of both "foundation" and "society," see Claus Fischer, "Bericht ...," *Jahrbuch* 1995, 267–73, 10n; and Heinz Wissenbach, "1995 ...," *Jahrbuch* 1996, 271–76. Regular reports have followed since then.

14. Ingrid Rosski, "Die Frauenkirche erhält Steine der Torgauer Brücke," *Dresdner Neueste Nachrichten*, November 8, 1994; and Reinhard Delau, "Torgaus Brückensteine für die Gewölbe," *Sächsische Zeitung*, February 16, 1996. The Torgau bridge had its own claim to historical importance, for it was on it that in 1945 American and Soviet troops met.

15. The art project was initiated in 1995 and pursued up to a point in consultation with Rainer Volp, a scholar of Lutheran theology and expert on contemporary Christian art. The project is documented at the Landesamt für Denkmalpflege Sachsen (IDS, DN Frauenkirche, 1994–; and DN Frauenkirche, Bauausschuß). For the other proposals, see *Sächsische Zeitung*, June 12, 1990; *Dresdner Neueste Nachrichten*, April 8, 1992; *Dresdner Neueste Nachrichten*, October 18, 1995; and *Die Kirche*, November 5, 1995. Hans Nadler explained his idea to me in conversation on April 18, 1996.

16. Reinhard Bentmann, "Die Fälscherzunft—Das Bild des Denkmalpflegers," in Wilfried Lipp, ed., *Denkmal—Werte—Gesellschaft*, 203–46, phrase cited, 244, 245. Bentmann also addresses the subject of inauthenticity, or of "designing" history, in "Geschichtsdesign," *Alles Design*, in *Kursbuch* 106 (1991), 33–51.

17. On Saxon sandstone and its properties, see Dieter Beeger, "Naturstein in Dresden," *Schriften des Staatlichen Museums für Mineralogie und Geologie zu Dresden* 4 (1992), 7–14.

18. The West German *Duden*, vol. 4, 1598–1600 (Mannheim, Vienna, and Zurich: Duden, 1978), defines *Kulturerbe* as a German translation of an originally Russian concept especially used in the GDR for the "inherited cultural property of a community, a people: national heritage." The East German *Wörterbuch der Gegenwartssprache*, vol. 3 (Berlin: Akademie-Verlag, 1969–1976), 2254–56, defines it as "inherited cultural property (of a people, a society)."

19. On *Wahrzeichen*, see Johann Heinrich Zedler, *Grosses vollständiges Universal-Lexicon...*. (Halle and Leipzig: Zedler, 1732–50), vol. 49, col. 1116, and vol. 51, col. 1064; Jacob and Wilhelm Grimm, *Wörterbuch der deutschen Sprache*, vol. 13 (Leipzig: S. Hirzel, 1922 [orig. 1854–]), cols. 1016–30. The Grimms include in their definition of *Wahrzeichen* the trace of something that no longer exists (col. 1025) as well as the intimation of something that does not yet fully exist (col. 1026). Both meanings apply to the postwar Frauenkirche, but have been lost in the contemporary usage of the term. See *Duden*, vol. 6, 2832; and *Wörterbuch*, vol. 6, 4240.

20. On the concept of *Erlebnisaesthetik*, see Hans Georg Gadamer, *Truth and Method*, 2nd rev. ed. , translated by Joel Weinheimer and David G. Marshall (New York: Continuum, 1996), 55–81.

D. MEDINA LASANSKY

BLURRED BOUNDARIES BETWEEN TOURISM AND HISTORY: THE CASE OF TUSCANY

Italy is the consummate tourist destination. The country's tourism industry, hundreds of years old, has undergone a constant process of refinement, continually finessing strategies of representation and mediation to the point that Italian sites are familiar throughout the world. In a popular contemporary tourist poster Italy is made up of iconic premodern structures—culled from various cities and collaged into a geographic relationship.

The Duomo in Milan is located next to the Certosa in Pavia, which is adjacent to the Palazzo dei Consoli in Gubbio, which is sited next to Portofino. The poster raises several questions. How has this canon of sites been determined, by whom, and for what end? What is the role played by the historian in the construction of this canon? To what extent is the historian's knowledge influenced by the mass media directed at tourists or by inherited touristic traditions? In other words, what has been the impact of tourism on the practice and production of history and place? How do the modes of interaction, ways of looking, and expectations of the historian and tourist affect one another?

The practices of both mass tourism and art and architectural history were born in the nineteenth century. This background continues to be reflected in the way in which these practices are carried out—in other words, in terms of how the tourism industry and historians look at and study sites and in how they contextualize these sites in historical terms. Within this framework, it is enlightening to examine the construction of the image of an "authentic" Tuscany—one of Italy's most visited regions. What sites constitute this image and how have they been narrativized for consumption?

Recently, the magazine *Bon Appétit,* which focuses on food and cooking, published a special issue dedicated to Tuscany. Twenty-five "traditional" dishes were prepared and photographed in some of the region's most scenic spots: *ribollita* in Siena, a fruit tart in Pisa, and *porchetta* against the backdrop of the medieval houses in the Piazza Grande in Arezzo. As the magazine's editors noted, "This is the Italy of our dreams—the magical region we have read about, seen in paintings and fantasized about…the medieval villages, walled towns and Renaissance cities. It is the land of Florence, Siena and Lucca, of the Uffizi and the Leaning Tower of Pisa and more Duomos than we can count. It is the home of Dante, Galileo, Machiavelli, Leonardo, Michelangelo.…"[1]

Bon Appétit's Tuscany is a familiar, beguiling place, made more so by the homey recipes of Florentine cook Lorenza de'Medici and the nostalgic prose of Frances Mayes, the best-selling author of *Under the Tuscan Sun*—two experts who have made successful careers out of capitalizing on the appeal of the region. Included are testimonials that somehow legitimize the authenticity of their project. Mayes quotes Maria "Mama" Rita, her neighbor Lucio, a pasta maker named Dino, and Giotto, the gardener, among others, as if to underscore the authority of her

voice through its proximity to the native informant.

In this image, food plays a central role. Cuisine is one of the most defining and saleable attributes of Italy today. There are countless guidebooks that feature food—some exclusively. The influential "slow food" movement was founded in 1989 to protect the "authentic" culinary culture of Italy from the invasion of fast food venues such as McDonalds. A new law has even been proposed to regulate the quality of the foods that have come to represent the region: olive oils, cheeses, and wines.

Today it would be hard to envision a trip to Italy without gastronomic pleasure. Those seeking the truly "authentic" vacation are now encouraged to pursue agritourism—a subculture of tourism in which food is central. Yet this has not always been the case. Food is notably absent from the late nineteenth- and early twentieth-century guidebooks and travel accounts. Mark Twain actually bemoaned the country's terrible cuisine in an irreverent chronicle of his "grand tour" entitled *The Innocents Abroad* (1869).

But, what does all this have to do with architecture? The fact that food is now a primary element in the image of an "authentic" Tuscany points up the malleability of what constitutes the authentic. It demonstrates that the authentic is a cultural construct that is in a constant state of flux and redefinition. It has less to do with past historical reality than with contemporary tastes, trends, and rhetoric, whether that rhetoric is political, economic, or something else. In the end, it is the need to continually monitor and contemporize the "authentic"

ITALIA: la più bella "città" del mondo

"Italy: the most beautiful 'city' in the world." Tourist poster promoting Italy.

(through refinement and redefinition) that ultimately generates and sustains tourism. Arguably, the same holds true for other aspects integral to the image of Tuscany, namely, Renaissance architecture. Like food, Renaissance architecture has been "authenticated" in contemporary terms at various times during the past centuries. The Fascist period in Italy provides a particularly illustrative example.

Our contemporary conception of the Tuscan Renaissance landscape, in both touristic and scholarly terms, is indebted to the machinations and designs of the Fascist government, evidenced by a range of sources—government correspondence, photographs, architectural drawings, and the ephemera of popular culture.[2] A guidebook published by the Italian government in 1931 describes Tuscany as the "cradle of medieval and Renaissance civilization."[3] As such, the region was widely considered the birthplace of *Italianità,* or Italianness. Mussolini's government found that by celebrating the Renaissance, it could reinforce the idea of a native Italian cultural and intellectual superiority—and in the process, strengthen contemporary political authority, which took on the legitimacy of an inherited and inalienable right. Eager to promote a shared sense of *Italianità,* the Fascist government encouraged Tuscan towns to "medievalize" their historic centers by restoring buildings, spaces, and rituals to their so-called "original" and "native" form. To achieve these ends, a range of structures were "liberated," "revived," "restored," and "purified."

At some sites this impulse also assumed a transitory form, as in the case of several Renaissance festivals. The famous *palio* in Siena (a horse race that took place around the perimeter of the main piazza), for example, was redesigned in 1928 by a committee of artists and historians to appear more "coherently medieval and distinctly Sienese."[4] Artisans and guild members were added to the *corteo,* or opening parade. In addition, participants were given new costumes that were inspired by the paintings of Benozzo Gozzoli and subjected to intense scrutiny by the advisory committee. It was argued that in its revised form the *palio* was more true to the period, or "authentic."

The regime's revisionist Renaissance history is most apparent, however, in its permanent physical form. Buildings were renovated to appear as they might have looked during the fourteenth or fifteenth centuries. Structures such as the town hall in Figline Valdarno were "liberated" from the detritus of post-Renaissance construction; and churches like that of San Michele and San Adriano in Arezzo were purged of their neoclassical facades and refaced in a more authentically medieval style.

In most cases the renovations fulfilled contemporary stereotypes regarding the Middle Ages and the Renaissance. In Arezzo, for example, the main piazza was redesigned, beginning in the late 1920s, to quote elements from neighboring (and better-known) Tuscan towns. The *cotto* (brickwork)

Local culinary dish on display in front of the Duomo of Massa Marittima. From *Bon Appétit,* May 2000.

paving imitates that of Siena, while the newly added well and medieval-style towers refer to San Gimignano. The city's town hall and bell tower were given a new facade to resemble those of the Palazzo Vecchio in Florence. Even the houses flanking the piazza (the same houses that were featured as a backdrop in the *Bon Appétit* article) were restored in a convincingly Renaissance style. In San Gimignano, a new fourteenth-century style loggia (following the style of the Loggia dei Lanzi in Florence) was incorporated in 1934 into the existing town hall; crenellations were added to the upper floors and the abutting tower was raised an additional story.

In some cases, entire towns were shielded from modern incursions altogether. In 1928 the walled city of San Gimignano was declared a "monument zone." The effect was that the Renaissance past was presented as the preeminent historical period, to be preserved at the cost of all others. Also at this time, it first became illegal to alter structures dating from the Renaissance.

These restoration projects were arbitrary at best. Rather than being based on archaeological or other research, they were intended to reinforce an ideal image of the past. By telescoping history, they gave the impression that the sites, or activities (in the case of the *palio*), were inherited uncorrupted and unchanged—that they had survived intact. This obviously was a forced reading, as these sites underwent continual change. The *palio*, for instance, while it has roots in the fourteenth century, had never actually been a Renaissance-style event (nor necessarily even a horse race). Typically, participants dressed in neoclassical fashion and on more than one occasion were seated on floats shaped to resemble Mount Parnassus.

Once reconstructed, the Tuscan landscape was then packaged and presented to the public. During the 1930s and early 1940s various forms of mass media were deployed to codify what we know today as "Tuscany." Film, photography, calendars, and tourism helped to choreograph both site and sight, teaching people what to look at and how to look. The intended audience was national rather than foreign.

Mussolini sought to reclaim the Italian Renaissance from the dominion of foreigners—tourists and scholars alike, focusing attention on institutions like the German Kunsthistorisches Institut (a center for art-historical research based in Florence) and individuals such as Edith Wharton (whose study on Italian Renaissance gardens was widely acclaimed). It was during the Fascist regime, in fact, that the term *turisti* (tourists) replaced that of *forestieri* (foreigners)—a metonymic change that conveys the government's interest in taking back the Italian Renaissance landscape for the Italian *popolo* from the foreign bourgeois audience that had served as its unofficial guardian for more than a century. Franco Zeffirelli's 1999 autobiographical film *Tea with Mussolini* captures the essence of this maneuver. In one scene a group of English and American women lounge comfortably on padded velvet chairs, sipping tea from fine china, against the backdrop of Leonardo da Vinci's painting *The Annunciation*. It is clear that they enjoy a privileged and intimate relationship with Renaissance art. The scene ends abruptly with the entrance of virile young Fascist Black Shirts who storm the gallery and order the stunned women to leave. The women resist, and the Black Shirts—with dramatic flair—throw the china out of the window and forcefully escort the ladies from the room.

By the 1930s, this reclamation was well underway. A six-day work week, a new highway system, and improved rail lines complete with frequent discount fares and sponsored excursions enabled the urban working classes to visit sites such as Siena, Arezzo, and San Gimignano for the first time. In the mid-1930s, more than 1,500 annual train trips were sponsored by the government, transporting eager visitors to small towns throughout the country.[5] These *pellegrinazioni* (pilgrimages) were designed to inspire a cult devoted to Tuscany, marking the beginning of what would become a standard Sunday afternoon activity for the average Italian citizen.

By amplifying certain sites and suppressing others, the various forms of National Fascist Party (PNF) media helped to structure a relationship between site,

history, and contemporary Italian identity that was dependent on a contemporary notion of the authentic past—one that emphasized civic architecture for public consumption. This revised version of the past was a participatory history that required an engaged audience. Working-class Italians were expected to familiarize themselves with the Renaissance past, which was presented as the foundation of the modern state. Tourism was thus defined as a patriotic duty and a cultivated activity.

Despite this official construct, there is no doubt today that the Fascist regime's redesign of sites such as Arezzo, San Gimignano, and Siena were built on misconceptions and preconceptions of the past. In many cases historical records provide evidence of the ways in which the design process was compromised to include items that, while believably authentic, were inaccurate. There is a distinction to be made nonetheless between the authentic and the accurate, as the medievalist Michael Camille noted in an interview for the radio program *This American Life* (1996). The interview was conducted while visiting a medieval theme restaurant located in a twentieth-century castle outside of Chicago, and Camille claimed that the experience, created by what can only be termed a "bad simulacrum," was, in fact, quite "authentic." According to Camille, the choreographed dinner entertainment, a joust, closely approximated an event from the Middle Ages in many ways. It was a lowbrow popular spectacle and, while many of the details were historically inaccurate (for example, commoners intermingled with nobles in the jousting arena), the event recreated the general spirit of the period. In this sense, it was more authentic than would have been possible had it been accurate. In other words, authenticity has more to do with the intangible experience than with anything else.[6]

In any case, it is the image of the authentic Tuscan landscape designed by Mussolini's government for Italian tourists that remains in use today. A contemporary advertisement for the airline Alitalia makes this point emphatically as it beckons would-be visitors to "Discover the soaring towers of San Gimignano, serene piazzas of Lucca, or noble pageantry of Siena." Although the tourist market is larger, and the rhetoric is no longer tied to Fascist agendas of cultural and racial superiority, Italy's present is still very much rooted in its past—in the case of Tuscany, its Renaissance past. This image of Tuscany is threatened by corruption from non-Tuscan products. Foreign competitors have begun to appropriate the region's picturesque scenery (the rolling hills, cypress-lined roads, and poppy fields) as if assuming that this landscape could impart a sense of quality, taste, and craftsmanship to a product that otherwise has no connection to Tuscany. To protect the "authentic" character of the region's image, the president of the Tuscan Federation has sought to copyright the Tuscan landscape, arguing that while pasta, *panforte,* and the Monte dei Paschi bank are acceptable Tuscan products, pantyhose, Volkswagens, and Lucent technologies are not. If the regional government has its way, it may soon become impossible to film commercials or photograph advertisements for foreign products against the backdrop of Tuscany.

What is notable is not that the image of Tuscany continues to thrive (it is an excellent product, after all), but that tourists, students, and scholars alike continue to seek out the "authentic" Tuscany as the center of the Renaissance, to the exclusion of all else. University students I have observed who take part in a junior year abroad program in Italy usually marvel at the Renaissance architecture in Florence: the Duomo, the Palazzo Signoria, the church of Santa Croce, and the city center filled with its impressive array of civic architecture. They are taught that there is something inherently more authentic about being on site. I would suggest, however, that their mode of viewing and discussing these sites is indebted above all to a Fascist telescopic vision. They are not taught that the Duomo, Santa Croce, and the city center are innovative nineteenth-century projects. Nor do they visit modern structures, such as Gruppo Toscano's Santa Maria Novella train station (1932–35) or Pier Luigi Nervi's stadium (1932). And when they report

back that they have witnessed the *palio*, they claim that they have seen a Renaissance event, not a Fascist version of a Renaissance event.

It thus becomes clear that, as taught and presented, Renaissance architectural history is guided by the notion that there is some way to isolate the Renaissance from all that has happened subsequently. There is the underlying assumption that buildings can be seen as distinct from one another, ripped from their evolutionary context, and sequestered, away from the multiple layers of history. Any other perspective would complicate the narrative. The result is that architectural history continues to sustain the idea of an architectural canon of monuments categorized by historical period. It may be more accurate in this particular case, in fact, to consider that what is commonly studied by historians and students as Renaissance architecture is in reality a nineteenth- and early twentieth-century conception of the Renaissance.

Contemporary historians readily admit that history is a product made and remade in a specific time and place that says more about the present than about the past. They acknowledge that the past is constantly being renarrated according to contemporary goals, rhetoric, and media. Yet, while it is easy to recognize how places such as, say, Las Vegas's Excalibur Hotel and Casino (designed by Veldon Simpson, 1990), which includes a restaurant called Lancellota Pasta, or commercial ventures such as the "Medieval Barbie" doll are well-choreographed historical pastiches, Renaissance Tuscany has remained immune to close scrutiny. It remains protected within an entrenched nostalgic and romanticized vision of the Italian past that appears to be more closely aligned with touristic practices than it is to contemporary historical agendas. As such, the Renaissance historian seems to resemble nothing so much as E. M. Forster's fictional character Lucy Honeychurch, guided by her Baedecker and recollections of Ruskin.

It is here—within the context of seeking out the authentic—that the boundaries between tourist and scholar blur. At the same time, it is clear that this impedes the telling of a responsible and transparent history that exposes its logic. Historians function under the pretense of revealing "accuracy," while in fact they are simply reifying the "authentic." They purport to practice something that is distinct from tourism and yet continue to be guided by it. In many ways, history is similar to the collage of images of sites on the poster described at the beginning of this essay. Monuments have been decontextualized and repositioned according to the trajectory of an overarching narrative. Not surprisingly, historians tend not to discuss how sites have changed—in physical form, meaning, and mediation—over time.

Perhaps historians can learn to be more self-reflective in terms of how and why we select projects, in order to more consciously disclose the way in which we practice and construct history. It is time to break through the disciplinary boundaries of geography, time, and medium that have thus far precluded architectural historians from diachronic discussions. If a discussion can emerge that addresses the way sites change and morph over time in terms of form, function, meaning, and consumption, a more fluid historical topography might result, one that takes into account the touristic experience.

NOTES

1. Introduction to Frances Mayes, "The Tuscan Table" *Bon Appétit*, May 2000, 115.

2. For a more extensive discussion of the Fascist-period rescripting of the Tuscan Renaissance landscape, see D. Medina Lasansky, *The Renaissance Perfected: Architecture, Spectacle, and Tourism in Fascist Italy* (University Park, Penna.: Pennsylvania State University Press, 2004).

3. E.N.I.T. [National Organization for Italian Tourism], *San Gimignano* (Rome: Pubblicazione dello Stato, 1931), n.p.

4. On the redesign of the festivals, see D. Medina Lasansky, "Tableau and Memory: The Fascist Revival of the Medieval/Renaissance Festival in Italy," *The European Legacy* 4, no.1 (1999), special issue entitled *Post-Modern Fascism*, guest-edited by Richard Bosworth.

5. Antonio Crispo, *Le Ferrovie Italiane. Storia Politica ed Economica* (Milan: Dott. A. Giuffrè, 1940), 284.

6. Michael Camille interviewed in a special broadcast of *This American Life* entitled "Simulated Worlds," produced by Ira Glass for WBEZ Chicago, October 11, 1996.

ANETTE BALDAUF
SELLING THE SHTETL

In 1993, Steven Spielberg's Holocaust movie *Schindler's List* put Kazimierz, a district in the Polish city of Krakow, onto the international tourist map. Because the director had filmed his ghetto scenes in Kazimierz, the old quarter became widely mistaken for the site of Krakow's wartime Jewish ghetto. In fact, Spielberg's choice of location relied on a poetic translation error: Kazimierz had actually been one of Poland's most vital Jewish districts, where more than 70,000 Jews had lived before the Nazi invasion of Krakow. After 1939, however, most of the population of Kazimierz was forcibly removed to a ghetto one kilometer across the Vistula River. All traces of this ghetto, and its horror, were erased following World War II by robust Communist housing projects and ostentatious glass palaces. Responding to this erasure, Spielberg set his depiction of displacement in Kazimierz.

In contemporary Kazimierz, cinematic narration and real-life stories, commerce and domesticity, compete relentlessly over space. In a city darkened by soot and freighted with history, every particle of daily life seems imbued with commemoration. Conflicts over whose history should be remembered, what heritage restored, and which artifacts recycled, saturate each and every negotiation.

After *Schindler's List* was released, tourism in Krakow increased by more than 80 percent.[1] Suddenly, businesses in Kazimierz recognized the commercial potential of a selectively composed past: the district's prewar history. That history arguably began in 1495, when King Jan Olbracht compelled the Jewish population to move into a walled-off area in Kazimierz after the Jews were blamed for a series of fires that had destroyed most of Krakow's Judenstrasse. During the next two centuries Kazimierz's humanism and

Renaissance guided all of European Jewry. The district was not administratively incorporated into Krakow until the end of the eighteenth century, however. In 1820 the walls were removed and Jews were invited to assimilate and choose their place of residence. By the end of the nineteenth century, Jewish society in Kazimierz had developed a complex social stratification, encompassing assimilated and Orthodox Jewry, Jewish political parties, and Zionist groups.[2]

Nonetheless, with the exception of the assimilated Jews living in the center of Krakow, Jews and Poles largely maintained a rigid differentiation of identities. Poignantly articulated in the metaphor of the stranger elaborated by the German sociologist Georg Simmel, Jews perceived themselves as part of a different people, passing through on the way to the promised land. Poland's nobility (*szlachta*) exploited this position early on by appropriating the Jewish middle class as a

buffer zone between the powerful and the less powerful, or virtually powerless groups. For a variety of reasons, including anti-Semitism, the lower strata constructed their identity as Poles in constitutive opposition to the Jews. As the historian Eva Hoffman has argued, the Jews were the Poles' radical Other, just as much as the reverse was also true.[3]

Today, the remnants of seven synagogues, a bathhouse, a market square, and a town hall assist visitors in their imagination of what life for Jews might have been before its destruction. The pre–World War II cultural and religious center of Jewish life has since the reopening of Poland evolved into a hub for Jewish-style commerce. Today the district's restaurants serve kosher food, local bars fill the air with klezmer music, and a sign in a well-stocked Jewish bookstore suggests, "Visit Sites from *Schindler's List.*" Tour guides direct innumerable tourists through the streets, intertwining

stories around locations from Spielberg's movie and World War II historic sites. Jewish signs and totems are overtly present in Kazimierz; the irony is that hardly any Jews still live there.

Of the five hundred fifty buildings in Kazimierz, five hundred are designated as historic.[4] Some, located on the main square, have refurbished facades evoking the golden age of the shtetl. Gaudily decorated, these structures feed off a hyperbolic Jewish iconography, a Jewishness writ large. In the midst of this renovated landscape, however, a few ruins—dilapidated, covered in ivy, and barricaded with wooden planks—insert an uncanny reminder of the past. This mix of rehabilitation and decay has its roots in a complex tangle of history and ownership issues. After the fall of the Iron Curtain, descendants of original Jewish home

Apartment block, Kazimierz, Poland, 2001. Photo: Pat Blashill

owners started to return to Kazimierz and reclaim the buildings that once had belonged to their families. The city of Krakow has since returned as many as twenty buildings per year to the families of former owners, who in some cases have put the properties back onto the real estate market.[5] Private investors, in turn, have stepped in to buy and then renovate most of the houses situated around the wide main square. Other buildings have not been touched in decades, mainly because their ownership remains unclear. In the late 1990s, the city of Krakow and several private real estate concerns completed the renovation of a handful of such buildings, only to lose their investment when the families of Jewish owners appeared and reclaimed the houses.[6] Since these incidents, uncleared houses have been taboo; no speculator dares to disturb their coat of eerie historicity.

Just a few months before *Schindler's List* had its first screening in Krakow, a team of expert consultants from Edinburgh, Berlin, and Krakow were commissioned to develop recommendations on how to capitalize on the quarter's economic potential and improve the residents' quality of life. With a few minor exceptions, the result, known as the Kazimierz Action Plan, had no impact on the district's subsequent development.[7] Without a coherent policy to ensure the neighborhood's composition, Kazimierz's recent evolution has been determined thus far by the precarious decision-making of individual business owners and a strong belief in the deregulation of the market.[8] The artistic milieu and so-called decay chic have attracted new bars, restaurants, cafés, and a wave of mostly young residents. Nevertheless, since Kazimierz's popularity rose in the slipstream of a Hollywood blockbuster, critics tend to suspect that the area has been profoundly affected by the movie that made it world-famous.

Idiosyncratically, the debates about *Schindler's List* and Kazimierz share a similar topography. Like the debate surrounding the film, discussion of Kazimierz falls into four main areas of contestation: the impact of the culture industry (kitsch and spectacles), the problem of narrative (compositional unity, motivation, linearity, and equilibrium), cinematic subjectivity (the addressee), and questions of representation. According to the film theorist Miriam Hansen, the most significant feature of the debate on the movie is its inconspicuous rehearsal of the old debate on modernism versus mass culture.[9] The German studies scholar Andreas Huyssen poignantly called this feature a compulsive *pas de deux*.[10] Typically, the arguments employed are restricted by binary oppositions—high versus low, art versus kitsch, inauthentic versus authentic, and cognitive versus affective.

The main goal of Spielberg's Holocaust drama was to transfer memory invested with affection, as the historian Alison Landsberg reveals. Thus, Spielberg's objective becomes intelligible in the movie's last scene, when actual survivors gather on Oskar Schindler's grave. Landsberg observes, "This moment stages what I take to be the agenda of the film—the transferring of authentic living memory from the body of a survivor to an individual who has no 'authentic' link to the particular past."[11] Prosthetic memories, she argues, are memories that are not organically based, but are nevertheless experienced with one's own body, and inform one's subjectivity. Because prosthetic memories imply mimetic engagement and empathy, they are, according to Landsberg, capable of countering what Fredric Jameson called postmodernism's waning of historicity—the loss of access to a coherent historical past and its replacement by a pastiche of pop images.

But in the absence of a significant number of Jews, is the enactment of Jewish-style traditions capable of facilitating insights into a living culture? Of the seventy thousand Jews who lived in Krakow in 1929, only six hundred survived the war. The trauma of the Holocaust was aggravated by continuous attacks on Jewish survivors in the immediate postwar period, including the notorious pogrom in Kielce and the lesser-known one in Krakow in 1946.[12] Most Jews fled the cemetery that Poland had become. Under the Communist regime a series of anti-Semitic campaigns completed the destruction of Jewish life.

Today, the official Jewish community organization in Kazimierz consists of approximately one hundred fifty people, most of whom are over sixty years old. On the other hand, even though some critics have dismissed Kazimierz as a fake shtetl, the simulation has proved to evoke some very real effects. Thousands of Jewish tourists visit Kazimierz every year. Orthodox Jews treat it as a pilgrimage site, Israeli schoolchildren study it as an example of original Jewish life and destructive death, Holocaust survivors revisit their homes, and secular Jews engage in history. Today, signs of Jewish culture displayed on Kazimierz's streets indicate everything from orthodox belief systems to cultural radicalism and cosmopolitan lifestyles. In this context, young members of the local community have begun to rediscover—or fabricate—their Jewish roots.[13] Sponsored by the U. S.–based Ronald S. Lauder Foundation, a small group of teenagers, guided by a rabbi, recently began what the sociologist Malgorzata Melchior has called a mission: being Jewish in Poland.[14] Together they study the Talmud three nights a week, and tentatively they are beginning to reconstruct the foundation of a religious community.

Local business owners claim that commercial Kazimierz revalidates Jewishness, and thereby facilitates a collective reflection on anti-Semitism. If this is anything other than an alibi for the appropriation of Jewish culture, then Kazimierz's authenticity, or lack of it, is the least problematic issue surrounding its recent imagineering. And if the prosthetic memory on display in Kazimierz is also a lived space, where Poles find a place to counter their collective amnesia and reimagine their past, then the issue is also a Polish one. With this in mind, the focus shifts from questions of authenticity to those of representation and narration. There can be little doubt that the recreation of the shtetl is a Polish fantasy; it nostalgically projects the image of a harmonious prewar coexistence of Poles and Jews. The selective reconstruction offers the prosthetic memory of a life-world, that in the course of its actual destruction has become a trope. In

addition to its literal meaning, which is derived from the Hebrew word *shot,* or town, *shtetl* also connotes a whole, mainly premodern way of life anchored in the communal worship of family, religion, and tradition. With attributes such as safety, warmth, and an orientation toward community ascribed to its form, the shtetl serves as a subtle antidote to modern modes of living—what Max Weber called the iron cage, welded by forces of modernization. In the course of the last decade, Poland's population has experienced, painfully, an accelerated increase of exactly these forces: rationalization, calculation, and commodification.

Contemporary Kazimierz has become the epitome of a multicultural and upscale way of life. Historically, however, the Jews who lived in Kazimierz before the war were rather poor; more affluent, assimilated Jews lived near the center of Krakow.[15] In the new Kazimierz, gentrification has nearly doubled some local real estate values since the mid-1990s. This

Israeli school tour of Kazimierz, Poland, 2001. Photo: Pat Blashill

phenomenon has brought about an extraordinarily ironic twist of fate: many of the Polish families who moved into Kazimierz after the Nazis expelled Jews now fear displacement because of the area's exhibited Jewishness. Labeled *Lumpenproletariat* by many inhabitants of Krakow, these residents are often dismissed as being incapable of playing any role in the new market-driven economy. As such, they have something in common with the prewar Jewish population of Krakow: the attribution of radical Otherness. Today, the Otherness of Kazimierz's *Lumpenproletariat* absorbs all the undesirable qualities that the new Poland wants to shed.

Kazimierz is not an open-air Holocaust Museum, nor an entertainment park. It is, on the contrary, a place where 15,000 people live, vote, and are attempting to shape a community according to their vision. Faced with Poland's political credo of deregulation, several grassroots organizations have tried to counter dominant market-driven politics by building alliances between old and new residential groups. In this respect, Kazimierz will continue to be a compelling test case in plurality and multiculturalism. It may also illustrate whether industries of prosthetic memory have any significance beyond their pure market value. The future, Andreas Huyssen predicts in his reflections on historical monuments, will not judge us for forgetting, but for remembering all too well and still not acting in accordance with those memories.[16]

NOTES

1. According to the Krakow Real Estate Institute Foundation, tourism increased from 1.3 to 2.3 million from 1992 to 1993. In 1993, a quarter of the tourists were foreigners; international tourism had increased by 100 percent since 1991. See *Introducing Krakow Economy and Business* (Krakow: Krakow Real Estate Institute Foundation, 1995), 16.

2. Eugeniusz Duda, The *Jews of Cracow*, translated by Ewa Basiura (Krakow: Wydawnictwo Hagada and Argona-Jarden Jewish Bookshop, 1999), 22–26.

3. Eva Hoffman, *Shtetl: The Life and Death of a Small Town and the World of Polish Jews* (New York: Mariner Books, 1998), 20–72.

4. *Introducing Krakow Economy and Business*, 8.

5. Official data is not available. Some sources claim that this occurred with three houses, while others insist that the number is five.

6. Since no exact data is available on this matter, these figures represent estimates provided by the Kazimierz Local Office and the local Jewish community.

7. As a result of the Action Plan, the city of Krakow established the Kazimierz Local Office. This joint project between the city and nongovernmental organizations (NGOs), headed by Malgorzata Walczak, advises tourists, coordinates various interest groups, and publishes the bilingual newsletter *Kazimierz Local Quarterly*. Malgorzata Walczak, "Kazimierz—Into the New Millennium," *Kazimierz Local Quarterly*, 2000–01, 1.

8. Roberta Brandes Gratz, *A Frog, a Wooden House, a Stream and a Trail: Ten Years of Community Revitalization in Central Europe: A Report for the Rockefeller Brothers Fund in Cooperation with the Conservation Fund* (New York: Rockefeller Brothers Fund, 2001), 23–24.

9. Miriam Hansen, "Schindler's List Is Not Shoah: Second Commandment, Popular Modernism and Public Memory," in Yosefa Loshitzky, ed., *Spielberg's Holocaust: Critical Perspectives on Schindler's List* (Bloomington, Ind.: Indiana University Press, 1997), 82.

10. Andreas Huyssen, *After the Great Divide: Modernism, Mass Culture, Postmodernism* (Bloomington, Ind.: Indiana University Press, 1986), 44–62.

11. Alison Landsberg, "America, the Holocaust, and the Mass Culture of Memory: Towards a Radical Politics of Empathy," *New German Critique* 71 (Spring–Summer 1997): 63–64.

12. Duda, *The Jews of Cracow*, 115.

13. The first reawakening of Jewish self-awareness developed within the liberal wing of the Catholic church and the political opposition movements of the 1980s. In 1988 a group of students organized around Janos Makuch introduced the first Jewish Culture Festival, a celebration that since has become a renowned annual proclamation of spiritual belonging. See Janos Makuch's introduction to the schedule for the eleventh Jewish Culture Festival in Krakow (2001).

14. Malgorzata Melchior, "A Community in Search of Its Identity: Timid Revival of Polish Jewry," *Le Monde Diplomatique*, February 2000, 9.

15. Henryk Halkowski, "Kazimierz Yesterday and Tomorrow," in Judaica Foundation, Center for Jewish Culture, *The Jews in Poland*, vol. 2 (Krakow: Jagiellonian University Printing House, 1999), 227–34. The Judaica Foundation proposed the institutionalization of a Center for Jewish Culture in the late 1980s; eventually, the center was founded on the site of a former house of prayer in 1993.

16. Andreas Huyssen, *Twilight Memories: Marking Time in a Culture of Amnesia* (New York and London: Routledge, 1995), 260.

DETOUR
OBERSALZBERG, GERMANY

In March 2005, a five-star luxury resort, part of the InterContinental hotel chain, opened in the alpine hamlet of Obersalzberg, Germany, near the Austrian border. Designed by the German architect Herbert Kochta, the sleek modernist-inspired hotel of steel, glass, and concrete is shaped like a horseshoe so that all of its 138 rooms have panoramic views of jaw-dropping Bavarian mountain scenery. Anticipated as an economic boon to the region, it boasts a New Age Spa and an American Bar, and bills itself, according to its Web site, as an "oasis of well-being" for an upscale clientele. The twist is that its location, on a mountainside just above the town of Berchtesgaden, also offered a haven for Adolf Hitler and many high-placed Nazis starting in 1933 and continuing until Hitler's death at the end of World War II. In this idyllic setting, Hitler wrote the second part of *Mein Kampf,* and built his Bavarian-style retreat, Berghof, from which would be plotted the Holocaust and the takeover of Europe.

Inevitably, the hotel chain's choice of location has inspired controversy, mostly focusing on the site and its history rather than the building. An Israeli newspaper adopted the name "Hotel Hitler" and many Jewish groups as well as some local residents have expressed outrage. Ironically, after Allied forces bombed the Nazi complex here in 1945, the U.S. military used the area as a ski and golf resort, only returning it to Germany in 1996. Defenders of the hotel have also pointed out that Berchtesgaden has been a tourist destination since the nineteenth century. The Bavarian government, which owns the surrounding land and finally approved the InterContinental Berchtesgaden, has been trying to come up with a responsible renovation of the area since the mid-to-late 1990s.

In 1999, the state of Bavaria mandated the creation of a documentation center, located near the new hotel, detailing the area's Nazi history. As a condition for permitting a hotel to be built, the government required that it be designed for well-to-do tourists, to discourage neo-Nazi pilgrimages. The hotel itself has trained its staff to answer questions about the site's Nazi connections, and give information on the documentation center in addition to the lake, the salt mines (for which Obersalzberg is named), and other tourist destinations. Finally, the nightstand drawer in each of the rooms contains a copy of *Deadly Utopia,* a book of text and photographs describing the Nazi-era horrors.

Above, Adolf Hitler's Berghof, Obersalzberg, Germany, as completed in 1936 and after bombing in 1945.

JAMES E. YOUNG
THE VENERATION OF RUINS IN THE LANDSCAPE OF HOLOCAUST MEMORY

When the killing stopped, only the sites remained, blood-soaked but otherwise mute. During their operation, the Nazi death camps, such as Auschwitz and Majdanek, and the destruction of people wrought there were one and the same: sites and events were bound together in their simultaneity. But with the passage of time, sites and events gradually became estranged from one another. While the sites of killing remained ever-present, all too real in their physical setting, time subtly interposed itself between place and its past. Events that occurred in another time seemed increasingly to belong to another world altogether. Only a deliberate act of memory could reconnect them, reinfuse the sites with a sense of their historical past.[1]

Nevertheless, the powerful allure of ruins persists, a near-mystical fascination with sites seemingly charged with the aura of events that once occurred there, as if the very molecules of such places still vibrated with the memory of their past. Some people claim to intuit this aura in sites touched by "history," usually those who already know something of the site's past, or who suspect that a site is somehow historical. Just as houses come to be "haunted" by the ghosts (memory, really) of their former occupants, the sites of destruction are haunted by the phantom of past events, no longer visibly apparent, but only remembered.

Nor is the sanctification of ruins entirely foreign to Jewish tradition. As the most sacred icon and memorial space in Judaism, the remnant of the Western Wall of the Second Temple in Jerusalem recalls the destruction of the Temple through its own fragmentary link to the historical event. Though many would argue that the Western Wall is holy because of its link to the Temple rather than its reference to the Temple's destruction, it is that destruction and the subsequent dispersion that Jews have traditionally bewailed, not its building.

Remnants of the historical past have long come to stand for the whole of events: in the ruins of ancient cities, in the relics displayed in museums, even in the remains of our ancestors, we recall entire civilizations with an eye toward understanding them.

Too often, however, these remnants are mistaken

for the events from which they have been torn: in coming to stand for the whole, a fragment is confused with it. Authentic historical artifacts are used not only to gesture toward the past, to move us toward its examination, but also to naturalize particular versions of the past. Pieces of charred brick, or a broken bone, seem to endow their arrangement in museums with the naturalness of their own forms. At such moments, we are invited to forget that memory itself is, after all, only a figurative reconstruction of the past, not its literal replication.

Modern memory may indeed be archival, as the historian Pierre Nora suggests, relying entirely on the materiality of the trace. But at least part of our current veneration of ruins and artifacts stems from the nineteenth-century belief that such objects embody the spirit of the people who made and used them. In this view, museum objects suggest themselves not only as remnants of the people to which they once belonged but also as traces of the values, ideas, and character of the time. In the subsequent fetishization of artifacts by curators, and of ruins by the "memory-tourist," however, we risk mistaking the piece for the whole, the implied whole for unmediated history. Moreover, our veneration of a place leads to its consecration as holy site, sacred and seemingly transcendent in its significance.

For by themselves, these sites of destruction lack what Nora has called "the will to remember."[2] That is, without a people's intention to remember, the ruins remain little more than inert pieces of the landscape, unsuffused with the meanings and significance created in our visits to them. Without the will to remember, Nora suggests, the place of memory, "created in the play of memory and history… becomes indistinguishable from the place of history."[3] In concert with his suggestion that such places of memory exist "only because of their capacity for metamorphosis," Nora's observations will cut two ways for our understanding of the "memorial camps" in Poland, including Majdanek and Auschwitz.

On the one hand, we are reminded that it was the state's initial move to preserve these ruins—its will to remember—that turned sites of historical destruction into "places of memory." On the other hand, we find that these sites of memory also begin to assume lives of their own, often as resistant to official memory as they are emblematic of it. Later generations visit memorials under new circumstances and invest them with new meanings. The result is an evolution in the memorial's significance, occurring in response to the new times and company in which the site finds itself.

At the end of April 1940, some six months after invading and occupying Poland, the Germans

Entry gate to Auschwitz–I concentration camp. Photo: James E. Young

reinforced and electrified the fences surrounding the Polish Army barracks in Oswiecim, a small half-Jewish town in Silesia, and erected guard towers, converting the base into *Konzentrationslager* (concentration camp) Auschwitz-I. Though some of the first gassings were carried out here, Auschwitz-I was intended initially as an internment camp for Polish political prisoners and eventually Russian POWs. Within the year, however, it was decided to expand the camp into separate labor and killing centers. For labor, the Germans built a sub-camp, Buna, near the rubber and petrol works at Monowice. For their massive extermination center, the Germans razed the Polish village of Brzezinka, three kilometers down the road from Auschwitz-I, and built a gigantic complex of barracks, gas chambers, crematoria, and burning pits—all fed by a rail spur diverted from the main line. Thus, what the Germans would call Birkenau was itself created on the site of a demolished village, its very foundation a bed of ruins. During the next four years, some 1.3 million people (90 percent Jews) were murdered and burned at Birkenau, their ashes plowed into the soil, dumped into small ponds, and scattered into the nearby Vistula River.[4] When we recall that the Germans had rounded up 250 local Jews from Oswiecim as slave laborers to build the camp there, we also realize that the memorial at Auschwitz-Birkenau was, in effect, built by the victims it would later commemorate.

Late in November 1944, with the Soviet Red Army approaching, the Germans evacuated Auschwitz, leaving the sick and dying behind and forcing the rest on deadly marches west. After dynamiting gas chambers and crematoria and setting several dozen barracks alight, the Germans fled. The ruins, littered with the dead and dying, were still smoldering when the first horse-mounted Red Army patrols arrived a few days later. To prevent the spread of disease, Soviet soldiers burned down several of the barracks at Birkenau; other quarters were dismantled by local Poles in search of building materials and firewood. In 1947, the Polish parliament declared that the rest of the camp would be "forever preserved as a memorial to the

martyrdom of the Polish nation and other peoples."[5]

A visitor's first sight of the memorials at Auschwitz and Majdanek can come as a shock: not because of the bloody horror conveyed, but because of their unexpected, even unseemly beauty. Saplings planted along their perimeters, intended to screen the Germans' crimes from view, now sway and toss in the wind. Local farmers, shouldering scythes, lead their families through waist-deep fields to cut and gather grass into great sheaves. Beyond their pastoral facade, however, these memorials are devastating in their impact, for they compel the visitor to accept the horrible fact that what they show is real. In both cases, the camps seem to have been preserved almost exactly as the Russians found them forty years ago (though, in fact, they are much altered). Guard towers, barbed wire, barracks, and crematoria—mythologized elsewhere—stand palpably intact. In contrast to memorials located away from the sites of destruction, the remnants here tend to collapse the distinction between themselves and what they evoke.

Crumbling crematoria and barracks invite visitors to mistake remnants of the past for events themselves, physical evidence of almost any accompanying explanations. If, as was the case until 1990, it is engraved in stone that "four million people suffered and died here," then this is what the ruins tend to corroborate. In the rhetoric of their ruins, these memorial sites seem not merely to gesture toward past events but also now suggest themselves

Railway entry at Birkenau concentration camp. Photo: James E. Young

as fragments of events, inviting us to mistake the debris of history for history itself.

In addition to the national pavilions at Auschwitz-I, two blocks are devoted to historical chronologies of events leading to the establishment of the camp. What most visitors remember from trips to the museum here, as well as to that at Majdanek, however, are the few moments spent before the huge glass-encased bins of artifacts: floor-to-ceiling piles of prosthetic limbs, eyeglasses, toothbrushes, suitcases, and the shorn hair of women. Keeping in mind the earlier discussion of museological remnants, we should consider what it is precisely that the sight of concentration camp artifacts awakens in viewers, whether it is a sense of history, of evidence, or a feeling of revulsion, grief, pity, or fear. That visitors respond more directly to objects than to verbalized concepts is clear. But beyond affect, what does our knowledge of these objects—a bent spoon, children's shoes, crusty striped uniforms—have to do with our knowledge of historical events?

More specifically, what do we understand of the killers and victims through the figure of their remains? In one way, all we see here can be construed as remnants of the killers and their deeds. The dynamited ruins of gas chambers at Birkenau, for example, recall not only the fact of the gas chambers but also the German attempt to destroy evidence of this fact—a monument both to events and to the guilt of the killers. But in a perversely ironic twist, these artifacts also force us to recall the victims as the Germans have remembered them to us, in the collected debris of a destroyed civilization.

By themselves, these remnants rise in a macabre dance of memorial ghosts. Armless sleeves, eyeless lenses, headless caps, footless shoes: victims are known only by their absence, by the moment of their destruction. In great loose piles, the remnants remind us not of the lives once animating them so much as the brokenness of lives, now scattered in fragments. For when the memory of a people and its past are reduced to the ragged bits and pieces of their belongings, memory of life itself is lost. Familial relationships are sundered and evidence of scholarly

achievements, community, and traditions vanishes. Nowhere among this debris do we find traces of what bound these people together into a civilization, a nation, a culture. Heaps of broken artifacts belie the interconnectedness of lives that actually made the victims a people, a collective whole. The sum of these dismembered fragments can never approach the whole of what was lost.

That a murdered people remains known in Holocaust museums anywhere by their scattered belongings and not by their spiritual works, that their lives should be recalled primarily through the images of their death, may be the ultimate travesty. These lives and the relationships between them are lost to the memory of ruins alone—and will be lost to subsequent generations who seek memory only in the rubble of the past. Indeed, by adopting such artifacts for their own memorial presentations, even the new museums in America and Europe risk perpetuating the very figures by which the killers themselves would have memorialized their Jewish victims.

In this view, museums, archives, and ruins may not house our "memory work" so much as displace it with claims of material evidence and proof. Memory work becomes unnecessary as long as the material fragment of events continues to function as witness-memorial. We may be delegating to the archivist the memory work that is ours alone, thereby allowing memorials to relieve us of the memory burden we should be carrying. The archivist's traditional veneration of the trace is tied directly to a need for proof and evidence of a particular past. But the archivist too often confuses proof that something existed with proof that it existed in a particular way, for seemingly self-evident reasons. When taken together with the viewers' emotional, intellectual, and ideological responses to these arranged artifacts, the museum's total text functions much as any other handcrafted work of art. And while the museum's and viewers' intentions are important here, beyond intention lie the actual consequences of such exhibitions: what has the viewer learned about a group of artifacts, about the history they represent? On exiting the museum, how do

visitors grasp their own lives and surroundings anew in light of a memorialized past?[6]

The problem is not our uncritical belief in the notion that a spatial juxtaposition of artifacts can produce understanding (it does, it must). Rather, it is our uncritical belief in the particular kind of understanding produced, naturalized by the artifacts themselves, parts of a seemingly "natural order." In confusing these ruins for the events they now represent, we lose sight of the fact that they are framed for us by curators in particular times and places. This critique may be made of all museums, in fact, and is not intended to discredit any given Holocaust museum. However, we must continue to remind ourselves that the historical meanings we find in museums may not be proved by artifacts, so much as generated by their organization.

For most people removed from the site, Auschwitz has come to exist primarily as symbol, its physical topography supplanted by historical significance. Little by little, time and memory have turned the ground here into sacred space, seemingly inviolable. It has become a place of the mind, an abstraction, a haunted idea. For the contemporary Poles of Oswiecim, however, it is also home—and this small fact continues to bear directly on the shape of memory one finds here. What happened at Auschwitz may also in fact be a memory for many local townspeople, but the rusting barbed wire, crumbling barracks, and busloads of tourists constitute something more: daily realities by which current lives are navigated.

Irena and Tadeusz Szymanski, curators of art at the State Museum here, lived until not long ago in Block 20 at Auschwitz, not far from where Tadeusz was interned during the war as a Polish political prisoner, a two-minute walk to work. The place was quieter than during wartime, and by Polish standards, the accommodations were adequate, with sturdy buildings and plenty of heat and water. With the double rows of barbed wire fences no longer electrified, Irena and Tadeusz could come and go as they pleased. It was possible that instead of being reminded of the past here, in fact, the Szymanskis were reminded they were now free to leave at will, a dark source of pleasure.

For neighboring farmers and villagers, time has turned the ruins at Auschwitz-Birkenau not into memorial symbol or sacred space, but into landscape. It is a refuge where a few local citizens, like the Szymanskis, have even lived and where others still come to cut hay, rest, or play. Young lovers stroll among the rubble in search of a secluded glen in which to spread a picnic lunch. Children ride bicycles into shaded birch groves where other children once waited for death. Teenagers fish quietly on the bank of a little pond behind the crematoria, its shallows still white with human ash. They mean no harm. The tourists' memory space is, after all, their city park and state preserve. Whether we like it or not, the local citizens become part of our memory here, reinforcing our own prejudices perhaps, feeding our distrust.

But in fact, we must also recognize that this awful place remains sacred only in the great distance between it and ourselves, between its past and our present. The site retains its symbolic power over us partly because we do not live here, because we must make this pilgrimage to memory. For those who call Auschwitz their home, there may be no choice: each day and its small chores are framed not merely in the remembered image of this place, but in its hard reality—life goes on. The Poles who live here today know this place in the context of current lives, jobs, and family. It is part of a larger place called Polska. By contrast, we memory-tourists tend to see not only Auschwitz through the lens of its miserable past but all of Poland through the image of Auschwitz itself.

In conclusion, I would like to describe briefly some of the deliberations that swirled around the ruins during the process of reconceiving the memorial at Auschwitz. In the early 1990s, I was a member of the International Auschwitz Council and also of the so-called Yarnton Group, a group of Jewish intellectuals asked by the Polish government to come to Krakow to advise it on how to remake the memorial at Auschwitz after the fall of the communist regime in Poland in 1989.[7] On one of our tours of Auschwitz-Birkenau's far reaches, our group had found unauthorized spontaneous markers blooming in the landscape. One such set of markers erected by

young Polish volunteers provoked astonished gasps from the group and then an incredulous shaking of heads: arrayed across a great green meadow, the site of former burning pits and mass graves where tons of human ashes had been buried, now stood large, white-painted Stars of David and crosses. In two instances, the young Poles had attempted to create a symbol of solidarity between Jewish and Polish victims of the Nazis by nailing Stars of David to the crosses, in effect, crucifying the Jewish star. Where these memorial-volunteers had hoped to perform an egalitarian "marriage" of Jewish and Christian symbols, Jewish eyes found an ironic and bitter reference to the martyrdom of Jews at Christian hands.

Inspired by such scenarios, we returned to the seminar room in Krakow, ready to resume our Yarnton discussions. On the one hand, all agreed that the grounds should remain preserved as they are, with a policy to prevent the further vandalization of Auschwitz-Birkenau—whether by well-meaning volunteers, or by tourists looking for souvenirs, or by American museums foraging for artifacts. In particular, the sawing in half and removal of one of the last remaining wooden barracks at Birkenau by the U.S. Holocaust Memorial Museum in Washington struck an especially raw nerve among the group. As a result, we reiterated our previous recommendation that nothing from the site be carted off, that none of the grounds be altered in any way, without the approval of the entire Auschwitz Council.

At the same time, several members of the group expressed intense uneasiness with the obsessive, almost fetishistic veneration of these same relics. A Yiddish and Hebrew literature scholar, David Roskies, for example, warned passionately that Jews not turn the relics of Auschwitz-Birkenau into so many Stations of the Cross. For the next hour, we debated whether to conserve such artifacts as historical evidence or as remnants of the past meant to evoke in visitors the sense of having been there. Do we let the ruins age gracefully, to show the ever-widening gulf of time between ourselves and the

past terror that took place on this spot? Or do we restore them to their historically accurate original forms to show what had been?

With all this in mind, it has grown clear that that any outline for official memory here must be, like memorials themselves, provisional. Indeed, the process itself served as a reminder that as much as we desire it, no memorial is really everlasting: each is shaped and understood in the context of its time and place, its meanings contingent on evolving political realities. Perhaps the wisest course, therefore, would be to build into the memorial at Auschwitz a capacity for change in new times and circumstances, to make explicit the kinds of meanings this site holds for us now, even as we make room for the new meanings this site will surely engender in the next generation. For once we make clear how many people died here, for what reasons, and at whose hands, it will be up to future rememberers to find their own significance in this past.

NOTES

1. This essay is adapted from parts of James E. Young, *The Texture of Memory: Holocaust Memorials and Meaning* (New Haven: Yale University Press, 1993).

2. Pierre Nora, "Between Memory and History: Les Lieux de Mémoire," translated by Marc Roudebush, *Representations* 26 (Spring 1989): 19.

3. Ibid.

4. For the beginnings of an architectural history of Auschwitz-Birkenau, see Robert Jan van Pelt and William Carroll, *Architectural Principles in the Age of Historicism* (New Haven and London: Yale University Press, 1991), 345–69. A full-length study of the architecture of Auschwitz by Robert Jan van Pelt is forthcoming.

5. Kazimierz Smolen, ed., *KL Auschwitz* (Warsaw: Krajowa Agencja Wydawnicza, 1980), 16.

6. For his earlier, invaluable discussion of artifacts in the museum, I am indebted to Eugenio Donato's "The Museum's Furnace: Notes toward a Contextual Reading of Bourvard and Pécuchet," in *Textual*

Strategies: Perspectives in Post-Structuralist Criticism (Ithaca, N.Y.: Cornell University Press, 1979). One passage in particular is worth recalling here in its entirety: "The set of objects the Museum displays is sustained only by the fiction that they somehow constitute a coherent representational universe. The fiction is that a repeated metonymic displacement of fragment for totality, object to label, series of objects to series of labels, can still produce a representation which is somehow adequate to a nonlinguistic universe. Such a fiction is the result of an uncritical belief in the notion that ordering and classifying, that is to say, the spatial juxtaposition of fragments, can produce a representational understanding of the world. Should the fiction disappear, there is nothing left of the Museum but 'bric-a-brac,' a heap of meaningless and valueless fragments of objects which are incapable of substituting themselves either metonymically for the original objects or metaphorically for their representations" (223).

7. For a fuller elaboration, see my article "The Future of Auschwitz," *Tikkun* 7 (November–December 1992): 31–33, 77.

LUCY R. LIPPARD
THE FALL

I know New Yorkers, and in fact the whole damn country, have been through an orgy of recall these last few years, but I can't resist adding another stone to the cairn of September 11 and using Black Tuesday to contextualize this essay. When the "Architourism" conference was still planned for November 2001—the fall that became a Fall to end all falls, the end of the year, the end of innocence, but not, alas, of arrogance—I started to think again about "tragic tourism," the title of a book chapter I'd written a few years before without guessing how close to home it would come.

The World Trade Center has always been a tourist destination—going up, staying up, coming down, now going up again, in another futuristic guise. Living in what became SoHo in the 1960s, I watched the World Trade Center go up, and in 2001, in New Mexico, over the radio, I heard it come down. I'll try to avoid the pieties. But there's no question that overnight the World Trade Center, in all its towering ugliness, became the most famous architectural site, or the most famous ruin, the most famous pit, in the world.

I was in the city a couple of weeks after the attack. I couldn't bear the voyeurism of being a tourist at Ground Zero, so the night we arrived, we just walked down West Broadway to Canal Street. SoHo was pretty much business as usual. But Canal was lined with emergency vehicles. Tribeca was pitch dark and deathly still. It was as if a chunk of lower Manhattan had simply been erased. A profound sense of absence. But below the blackness, the site itself was fully illuminated by a harsh white light, where the crews were at work. The light at the end of the tunnel, since then transformed into ghostly towers of light.

Tourist, You Are the Terrorist!!, graffiti in Barcelona, Spain. Photo: L. R. Lippard

By the time I came back to New York in February, it was just a hole. A hole in the national psyche that had replaced earlier national ground zeros—the Trinity site in New Mexico, and the core of the Nevada Test Site. For some time now, we've been living in increasingly porous borderlands, but this hole is compelling on another level altogether. Inspired by my rural neighborhood in New Mexico, I had been writing about excavations and erections, the gravel pit as the rural industrial source and antithesis of the urban and symbolically postindustrial skyscraper and its archaeological parallels. In a rural context the gravel pit imitates nature. In an urban context the pit represents both destruction and construction, the rapid movement and change that characterize city life. September 11 speeded up the process, charged the meanings, undermined our social assumptions of invulnerability. For me personally, the gravel pit offers a metaphor for two extremes of the twenty-first-century cultural landscape, two of my own places—New York City, where I was born and spent most of my life, and a tiny village in New Mexico threatened by sprawl, where I've lived for ten years.

Saidiya Hartman recommends reinterpreting history by "illuminating the terror of the mundane rather than exploiting the shocking spectacle." As ruins, gravel pits are decidedly unspectacular. Nobody goes to see them. Their emptiness, their nakedness, their rawness, suggests an alienation of land and culture. Gravel pits are graves. And like graves they are often abandoned. Fresh Kills Landfill, before September 11 poised to become an outdoor art site, became a grave as well.

For all the mindless future that fuels the gravel industry, hidden evidence of the distant past, everything from dinosaur bones to stone tools, to industrial artifacts, to recent garbage, to nuclear waste lies buried in these pits. Salvage archaeologists working with highway departments find themselves on the front lines. And the pits may become tourist destinations. My favorite example is the ironic series of time lapses that are the history of Blackwater Draw in eastern New Mexico. The site of major discoveries for paleontology and archaeology in the 1920s, these were ignored until the 1930s, when the site was being used as a gravel pit and still more extraordinary artifacts came to light. Avid scholarship and excavations followed. Then the pendulum swung again and in the post–World War II highway boom, the archaeological site was reburied so it could become one of the state's largest gravel pits. And now, in another turnaround, what's left of it is a national historic site with a small museum, a very modest tourist destination banned by local Christian fundamentalists because of its Darwinian implications.

For a lot of people, gravel pits also represent pure potential as the bedrock of skyscrapers and the backbones of highways. If the modern city is vertical (a climb, leading to a privileged overview), the landscape of the American West is predominantly horizontal (a walk, through

Gravel pit in Nevada. Photo: L. R. Lippard

all walks of life), an extended construction leading to the city. Like the picture window, the road tantalizes and seduces, inviting invasion of previously wild or private places, paradoxically urging us to follow others in search of solitude. Gravel and travel are symbiotic.

The conflict between spectacle and engagement is heightened at the site of tragedy, mediated by awe if the site itself is visually overwhelming. Tourism is, after all, a visual art. It's about detail, about filling in the blanks, about seeing for yourself. If people travel to find what is missing in their daily lives, the grandeur of tragedy is oddly right up near the head of the list. Since September 11, gawking at Ground Zero is called patriotism. Our national propensity for denial has been overtaken by history and we don't know how to handle such a thing. Oddly enough, New York City, hitherto mistrusted and disliked by many Americans who think it's only a nice place to visit, now epitomizes America. The wounded Pentagon, embedded in the national corridors of power, is a hole, not an erection, and turned out to be merely the stepchild in this catastrophe.

Tragic tourism is a worldwide obsession. Are these our sacred sites? Are we drawn to such places by prurience, fear, curiosity, mortality (there but for the grace of god go I) or delusion (it can't happen to me—a peculiarly American sentiment, now to some extent outdated)? We visit such sites to get a whiff of catastrophe, to rub a bit closer to disaster than is possible in television, movies, or novels—although the imagination has to work a little harder when confronted with the pits, the blank terrains, the empty rooms, the neatly mowed lawns, the negligible remains of real tragedy. At these tragic sites, these communal *mementi mori,* we would do better to consider the society that produced them, the pits our president has landed us in today.

Tragic tourism, more than any other branch of the industry, raises the question of motivation, which mutually affects our views of history. Why is this building a ruin? Why is that one so emblematic that it has been tarted up and plaqued? Why is this landscape mined and clear-cut and that one an official wilderness? What are the local and global forces behind such choices? Public memorials and visited sites are the battlegrounds in a life-and-death struggle between memory, denial, and repression, not to mention contemporary ideologies. For obvious reasons, nonideological memorials are the most popular markers of any tragedy. In this country, where ruins are for the most part rare and picturesque, imparting nostalgia and moral lessons, cultural geographer J. B. Jackson has written, history is "a dramatic discontinuity," giving rise to "the necessity for ruins" which provide the incentive for restoration, a return to social origins, "a born-again landscape."

Monuments can exorcise memories as well as reinforce them. Repeated ritual at a site can offer periodic catharsis and eventual boredom. Monuments can serve as reliquaries,

Top, Steve Cagan, abandoned factory, Cleveland, early 1980s.

Bottom, Charles Simonds, *Excavated Inhabited Railroad Tunnel Remains and Ritual Cairns Below,* Niagara Gorge, Artpark, Lewiston, N.Y., 1974.

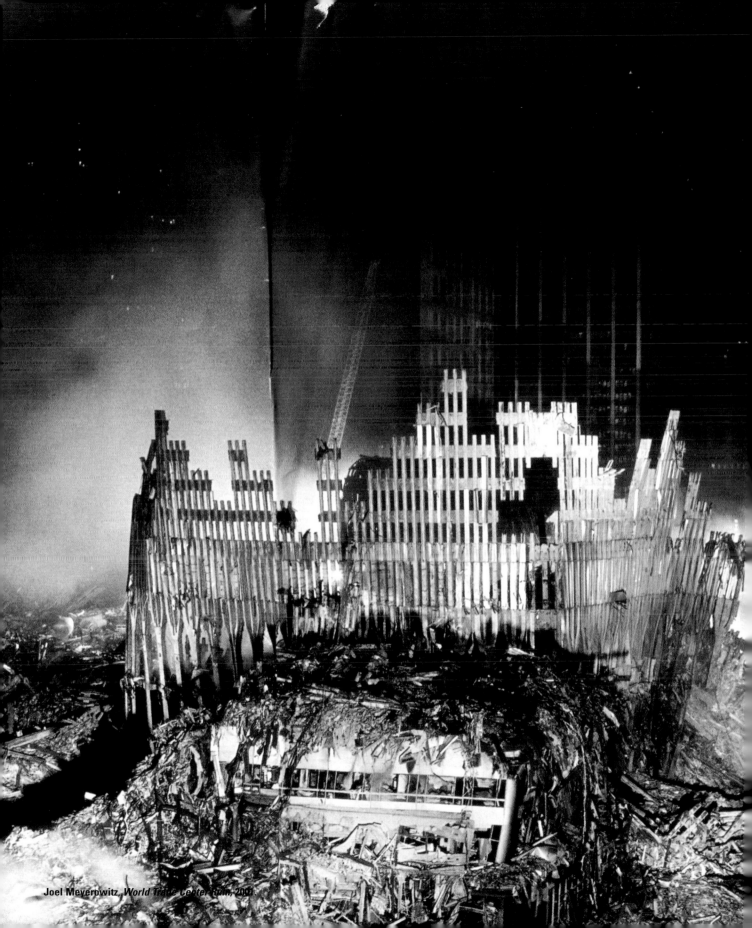

Joel Meyerowitz, *World Trade Center Ruin*, 2001.

repositories for memories we prefer not to carry around with us. In his brilliant book *The Texture of Memory,* James E. Young writes: "To the extent that we encourage monuments to do our memory-work for us, we have become that much more forgetful." Recently (but before September 11) Rebecca Solnit wrote similarly: "Eradicating the ruins can function as an urban lobotomy, erasing memory and dream, and rationalist amnesia is the current mental illness of American cities..."

In the United States, it often seems that memories of mass suffering are the morose keys to identity politics. Location, ownership, audience, agenda, agency, and commitment are pertinent factors. Consider what, if any, monuments we know to slavery, Native American genocide, Jewish holocaust, Irish famine, Japanese internment, Latino labor exploitation and deportation. A large number of Muslims were killed in the towers' collapse. How will that fact, and the deaths of unknown undocumented workers be memorialized? How much is cross-cultural understanding aided by these uneasy tourist moments? Do they divide and conquer, setting up a kind of competitive victimization? Young suggests the hopeful possibility of a "coalition of consciousness," memorials that include all horrors, so that, as he puts it, "every group in America may eventually come to recall its past in light of another group's historical memory, each coming to know more about their compatriots' experiences in light of their own remembered past." But such a monument might be so diffuse that it would lose the detail of place and narrative on which tragic tourism so profoundly depends.

While September 11 pales in comparison with losses suffered in other parts of the world, it's the worst single disaster on American soil, and we think big when it's our own tragedy. (On the other hand, the only monument at the Trinity site in New Mexico, where the world's first atomic bomb was detonated, a site that's globally far more significant—and only open to tourists twice a year—is a little stone park-service-type obelisk.) Size was of course the primary virtue of the Twin Towers. As Paul Goldberger has remarked, "When the biggest things in a city that prizes bigness becomes the most fragile thing, and the void has more weight than the solid, the rules of city change."

The modest, almost abject, monument at the Trinity site is a glued-together cairn, or stone pile. Cairns are the oldest known human mode of memorializing. Communal and participatory, they grow organically, measuring stone by stone the extent of loss. They are more likely to be destroyed by diffusion than by disaster, recycled for other uses when the original one is forgotten. But the World Trade Center fell suddenly, compacting time, changing our sense of time and scale. Instant symbolism. And at only twenty-eight years old—youthful cannon fodder. The touted "closure" so desired by our national pop psyche runs up against "Lest We Forget."

Most of the images I chose for my initial take on tragic tourism were public and architectural in the institutional or vernacular sense—a gas chamber at Dachau, a public school invaded by a gunman, an inner-city wall embellished with a murdered girl's face. Architecture establishes borders and social control, as in airports, courtrooms, gated

communities. When that fails, architecture contains and intensifies the narrative, makes it more tangible, more intimate, more ordinary, more tragic because it pinpoints the spot. You are here where it happened…. Enclosed graveyards exacerbate the sense of proximity to the dead. But a battlefield, an event, might be most poignantly memorialized by clusters of graves, huddled or isolated deaths becoming landmarks like the trees and hillocks and streams where the events took place, rather than by the deindividualized rows of identical stones in military cemeteries that some find so powerful.

Although Drex Brooks's photos of historic massacre sites as they look today—those ordinary but loaded landscapes, pastures, and suburbs—are incredibly haunting, they eventually allow the story to escape into surrounding spaces. This may be why we don't yet commemorate our eco-tragedies (soon to become overwhelming)—the lost rivers, creatures, forests, and grasslands. Their boundaries are too vague, and too huge, to take in. Tours might be the most effective memorials here. But a flippant article in the *New York Times* (June 2002) proclaimed that "Ecotours are so yesterday; architours are today."

Each tragic site has its own local context and character, its own landscape. Each site is heavy with associations and fantasies that will have a different impact on different groups and individuals as it changes context. The subtleties lie in gauging the power of what remains, physically and informationally, and its relationship to the cultural landscape in which it stands. Can we better picture what it was like to be there through detailed documentation, or through our own imaginations piqued by place? For me, an empty unmowed field with a forlorn and weathered marker (the Ludlow Massacre site in Colorado, for instance) is more evocative than an antiseptically manicured lawn with an elaborate monument. The weed-choked Jewish cemeteries in Poland may be more impressive than the official commemorations because their neglect continues as testimony to an anti-Semitism that has not died. And in turn, the ugly ruins of Jenin, of Afghan or Kurdish villages, speak far more forcefully of loss than will a handsome marble pile or a black box in the future.

Lest we disregard the power of ruins even as backdrop, consider Frank Gehry's horror at the possibility that the harsh industrial wastelands in Bilbao that now offer the perfect foil for his "metallic flower" might be "strategically beautified," dragging his building into a surrounding, a transforming, banality. The nature of the "new powerful myth" provided by Gehry's building depends, as Joseba Zulaika points out, upon "how it relates to the allegories cast by the city's ruins." Bilbao's future is a cliffhanger. Will this single art object coopt the fate of a whole urban landscape? If the trite beauty wins out, will the museum age well? What will it look like as a ruin?

Top, Alfred "Per" Oyaque and Omar "Nomad" Severiz, *Rest in Peace, Suly,* The Bronx, New York, 1993. Photo: Martha Cooper

Bottom, Rigo, *One Tree,* 1995. On-ramp next to freeway, San Francisco, California.

REST · IN · PEACE ″SULY″

11-27-76 · · · 5-28-93 · · ·

IN THE STREETS
OF CRIME, OUR YOUNG
BROTHERS DON'T THINK
THE TIME! GUNS DRAW A
BATTLE FIELD WE WEB!!
WHEN WILL WE CONSIDER OUR
OWN BLOOD SHED!
NOW THE INNOCENT PAY THE
TOLL WITH THEIR LIVES OUT
OF CONTROL. THE MASTERS
HAND NOW WE REST
HOPING + PRAYING THERE
WON'T BE A NEXT.

ONE TREE

The highway to Cerro Colorado near Galisteo, New Mexico, 2001. The hill in the background is both a pit and a (natural) erection. Its summit is a large quarry where the stone for the Cathedral of St. Francis in Santa Fe was mined. Photo: L. R. Lippard

More recently we have had the battle over how to memorialize the Twin Towers, and how to rebuild, whether to continue to fetishize the tragedy and focus on material culture or transcend and dematerialize, to focus less on the architectural object than on the ambiance of the whole, while avoiding what has been called *topolatry,* an insidious worship of place for the wrong reasons. What kind of permanent memorial can possibly extend to the ramifications of September 11's attack—not just the number of dead, or the pervasive fear, but the chauvinism, the xenophobia, the attacks on democracy ironically mounted in the name of democracy, on freedom in the name of freedom? The visceral power of the populist response, the shrines and photos, have been universally acknowledged. But taken out of their street contexts and exploited as high art they become poor substitutes for the tragedy they originally represented so well.

Tragedy is messy. The World Trade Center was neat. The pit has now been restored to neatness but the mess was the real message. We will probably be deprived of our ruin, and perhaps of our tragedy as well. As Susana Torre has written: "To build a new World Trade Center on the ruins of the old would be to pretend that what happened never did." It's time to rediscover the unspectacular, to create a counterspace, perhaps to incorporate the Islamic sense of the sacred void, or dare to imagine a truly civic space.

The first round of hackneyed proposals for rebuilding the Trade Center—happily rejected—hardly reflected the false and melodramatic rhetoric about Everything Has Changed since September 11. In fact the scariest thing is how little in this country has changed. The sacred economy is already fueling a new set of icons to commerce. I'd hoped the fall, tragic as it was, would serve some purpose, open up some crack in the system through which a new kind of visual activism would bubble up. A new humility, a new capacity to imagine a different way to continue—in the arts, and in tourism, which bears the commercial responsibility for commemoration. If we can't imagine a different future, a different site, and a different agenda, then we're doomed to build more ugly towers and get them shot down, literally or figuratively, again and again.

NOTE
1. This text was originally written as a lecture accompanied by some fifty slide pairs, which formed a parallel visual narrative. It has been cut and revised for the present publication. A few passages first appeared in *On the Beaten Track: Tourism and Place* (New York: The New Press, 1999) and in "A Crack in the System," *Andover Bulletin* 33 (Winter 2002).

HANS HAACKE
UNTITLED (WORLD TRADE CENTER)

2001—02
Die-cut white paper, 36 x 24 inches
Production: Creative Time, New York

In March 2002, at over 110 locations in Manhattan, poster-size paper
from which the silhouette of the World Trade Center had been cut out
was pasted over posters whose space rental had expired.

World Trade Center, New York, 1979.

TSENG KWONG CHI
SELF-PORTRAITS

1979–90
Gelatin silver prints
Courtesy Estate of Tseng Kwong Chi and Muna Tseng Dance Projects

These self-portraits with architectural icons, from a series entitled *East Meets West*,
parody stereotypes of travel photography and mass tourism. A self-proclaimed
"ambiguous ambassador" and an ambivalent citizen of the world, the Hong Kong-born
photographer began this project in 1979. He continued to work on it until his death in 1990.

Golden Gate Bridge, San Francisco, 1979.

Colosseum, Rome, 1989.

Chamber of Deputies, Brasília, 1984.

EXOTIC

The trope of the exotic persists in causing a level of intellectual discomfort, and rightly so. It typically operates, rhetorically, within a constellation of nation, displacement, desire, spectacle, and difference while in the service of a problematic formulation of alterity and its consumption. Since in many regards the exotic does not constitute an "encounter" with alterity, but functions instead according to a distinct mode of fantasy, we need first to ask, "exotic for whom?" Whether out of place or experienced away from home, things or people commonly referred to as "exotic" have probably not raised any specter of threat or contestation. The refugee or the *sans-papier,* for instance, is unlikely to be thought of as exotic. While the very possibility of experiencing something as exotic has, in any case, been challenged by the multiple forces of diaspora (including transnational economies and postnational identities), emerging geopolitical situations and technologies of globalization also, uncannily, seem to proliferate a longing for such outdated ideas about difference, especially within the tourist industry. Architecture as a destination for tourism is no exception.

On account of this situation it seems important to investigate whether the remaining discomfort of the term might harbor a potential "use-value" for the exotic, some scope for irony or contestatory practices in the engagement of such desire to other ends. The recent Tikki bar phenomenon in cities like New York and Los Angeles, among others, reminds me of a distinctly anticapitalist deployment of the exotic in the work of Jack Smith. While best known for films such as *Flaming Creatures,* from the early 1960s, Smith claimed the renovation of his East Village apartment—also done in the "exotic" style of orientalizing 1940s Hollywood movies—to be his most important work. As artist Mike Kelley has argued in his essay "Cross-Gender/Cross-Genre," distinguishing Smith's camp aesthetic from that of hippie culture, it is precisely the phoniness of Smith's appropriation of non-Western cultures that sets him apart from the essentializing logic of hippiedom, with its "exotic clichés—media-derived stereotypes of the Native American, the Indian mystic, and so on." While Smith's ironic appropriation raises other potential traps, it importantly stakes out politicized strategies of producing difference through other modes of identification.

Architecture that elicits touristic desire for the "exotic," whether as a result of national or vernacular particularity, typically functions semantically: one "reads" cultural meaning. This raises the question of whether more self-conscious relations to the "exotic" (whether ironic appropriation or less semantically defined forms of practice) could offer modes of identification that might, in turn, seek other political vocations in the present condition of diaspora. There remains a sense in which the exotic counters the universalizing logic of modernization. Yet in principle the particularity of the exotic arises not only out of an essentialist relation to place but also out of the specificity of displacement. Hence, this intersection of architecture and a term as problematic as *exotic* offers a fascinating site for an aesthetic-political investigation, one that might engage the many sides of current debates on cosmopolitanism—from critiques of the lack of responsibility of the cosmopolitan subject (those who disavow or lose their rights as citizens), to forms of political engagement that exceed nation-bound paradigms.

FELICITY D. SCOTT

MARC AUGÉ
CONTEMPORARY TOURIST EXPERIENCE AS MISE-EN-SCÈNE

Travel agencies are the true museums of today. In them one finds posters, brochures, films, and photos, and now virtual tours and visits to natural, urban, archaeological, and historic sites throughout the world. This vast amalgamation of information is characteristic of the general spirit of the early twenty-first century. Its effect is to put everything into the present time. We are no longer in an evolutionist period when traveling in space can be considered traveling in time; or when the peasants of Great Britain, for example, can be considered to be "survivals" of a more savage stage of civilization and, in this sense, as ancestors of the aristocratic or middle-class elite (as the nineteenth-century anthropologist Edward B. Tylor once claimed). Nowadays, all cultural, artistic, and ethnological manifestations appear as contemporaneous facts. This perception corresponds at the aesthetic level to what Francis Fukuyama has called "the end of history" in the political and economic domain.

This sense of contemporaneity adapts everything to the stage, so to speak. In French one would call it *mise-en-scène* or *mise-en-spectacle*. The diversity of the present reveals its full meaning at the global scale. The world is a scene or a show for those who have the means to travel through it. For those who do not, there is television. The French Hellenist J. P. Vernant, in writing about ancient Greek religion, touched on a paradox: religion was never so plausible, never such an important component of Greek urban identity, as when the Greeks considered it to be fiction, that is to say, as a set of theatrical scenes and narratives

pleasant to look at and listen to regardless of their historical or metaphysical truth. In our own society of spectacle and consumption, we may observe a similar transition from religion to theater. For instance, African groups perform with great talent in theaters throughout the world today, but their dances are completely cut off from the socio-religious context

I. M. Pei, addition to the Louvre Museum, Paris, 1989. Hundreds of visitors line up outside of the pyramid entry to the museum. Photo: Lionel Cironneau, AP Photo

from which they used to derive their meaning. The same is true of Afro-Brazilian Candomble, except for the fact that tourists often travel to Brazil themselves in order to be present at the Candomble scene.

The meaning of this contemporaneity can only be found, as noted, at the global scale. Formerly, travelers used to go to places situated along very precise religious or cultural itineraries. That was the case, for example, with sites like Mont Saint-Michel and Santiago de Compostela. By the 1950s, such places as Kathmandou shared the same status even though they belonged to a different ideological context. As for the intellectual and

cultural tradition, it too had its proper itineraries. Very often its destinations were, and still are, ruins—Greek, Egyptian, Roman, Mayan. For the young nineteenth-century European bourgeois gentleman, the Grand Tour to Rome, Athens, and sometimes the Middle East (the *voyage en Orient*) was a must. We may think of Chateaubriand, Flaubert, or even, a little later, Freud. For all of them, travel was an opportunity for a triple experience: to return to sources; to reflect on time and history; and to engage in self-reflection. In the nineteenth century, travel afforded an opportunity to construct identity through an encounter with

Tourists meditate at the archaeological site of Teotihuacan, Mexico, 1998. Photo: Marco Ugarte, AP Photo

alterity: with other peoples, other places, other surroundings and milieus.

Such places have not disappeared today, nor have the motivations of those who wish to visit them. But another type of privileged place has begun to supplant them, and within this context, the traditional pilgrimage sites have reappeared on the world stage as little different from the new ones. In the terminology and analysis of Rem Koolhaas, "historic" cities have now also become "generic." All places, all the remarkable sites in the world today, present themselves as goods for consumption.

These places are characterized by two salient features: singularities and images. By singularities I mean the qualities associated with such recently built places as the Guggenheim Museum in Bilbao, the Pyramid at the Louvre, or the Petronas Towers in Kuala Lumpur, all of which have come to be known as the work of a single artist despite the fact that many people contributed to their construction. These are signature buildings in the sense of the great paintings of Rembrandt or Titian. But they are also singularities in that they are situated in one place, one town, one country. They become identified with their location even though they are never truly representative or metonymic of this local context.

When one speaks of Frank Gehry's museum in Bilbao, one is not really thinking about the town of Bilbao or the Basque Country or Spain. Nor does I. M. Pei's Pyramid evoke Paris in the same way as does the Eiffel Tower or Notre-Dame. The work is singular, pure shape. It cannot be defined by its function. Who knows what is to be seen inside the museum in Bilbao? The Pyramid is the main entrance to the Louvre, but it could just as well be the entrance to a shopping center or railway station.

Rather, these buildings are singularities within the tourist network that, just like the economic and cybernetic networks, defines the contemporary world. These three networks—tourist, economic, cybernetic—are, in fact, partly overlapping. They have in common the fact that they extend over the entire world, but in a "lacunal" way: they have many gaps, and the result is a clear distinction between those places that are part of the "system" and those that are not.

At the same time, these singular places are also images. We get to know them long before we see them in reality (supposing we actually get the opportunity to do so). The technological network multiplies their images. It also multiplies the older images, those of the places that formerly were situated along the religious and cultural tourist itineraries. Now, however, we learn to recognize rather than to know them, despite guidebooks and a plethora of information. Recognition is more important than knowledge.

We may take ruins as an example. Take a site in, say, Mexico or Cambodia. We know, in fact, that only a very small portion of the total site has been cleared. We also know that every ruin is an amalgam of different periods; as in Rome or Athens, it represents a choice by archaeologists about what slice of time should be shown. As a result, what we are looking at is really just the spectacle of ruins. Especially when they are illuminated, as is so often the case in France, we are looking at a scene constructed in and for the present time.

We may summarize the above arguments as follows. Four principal shifts have occurred in our perception of the major tourist places today:
the network has replaced the itinerary;
the present has replaced history;
the singularity has replaced the symbol;
consumption has replaced experience.

McKENZIE WARK
MULTITUDES ON TOUR

Obsessed, bewildered

By the shipwreck
Of the singular

We have chosen the meaning
Of being numerous.

—George Oppen

There is a hotel shaped like a crocodile. It's in the Kakadu National Park, in the Northern Territory of Australia. You can stay there for A\$169 a night— in the off-season. The crocodile shape might refer to any of the things that one might journey there to experience. There are the Nourlangie and Ubirr Aboriginal rock art galleries. There is the Yellow Water Billabong and the massive sandstone escarpments above it. There are, in other words, all flavors of what was once the "exotic"—animal, vegetable, and mineral.

The exotic is what hails us from an elsewhere. It's a spatial notion, and since architecture as a discourse makes itself at home in all things spatial, it comes as no surprise that the exotic is a recurring point of reference for architecture—especially for the architecture of tourism. But there's a problem. It also should come as no surprise that the exotic, as such, in itself, no longer really exists. There is no place outside. The whole space of the planet is "inside." There are only interiors. The space of exploration is closed.

This is not a new proposition. But what might push it a bit further is to turn it around, and consider its consequences for architecture. What if, in the extinction of the exotic, architecture also ceased to exist? Can there be an architecture without an elsewhere, a pole against which it can ground its edifice? I think not. And so, rather than seeing the Gagudju Crocodile Holiday Inn as the epitome of an exotic architecture, or architecture of the exotic, it is rather the end of architecture and the beginning of something else, some other way of building.

It's common in thinking about architecture to think of it historically, as a succession of styles. Or perhaps one could say it is a succession of built relations to the passage of time. Not only European architecture has this historical consciousness. Postcolonial architectures also grapple with the form they might give to the beginning of new, modern, built histories. They construct their own historical forms parallel to

European architecture's historical times.

Indeed, what is postcolonial architecture but an attempt to commandeer, and overcome, the status of the exotic? Starting from exoticism, it recenters building on what was once consigned to the status of the peripheral. It makes a claim for a new centrality. This was the first, rather slow and incomplete way in which the exotic began to disappear—under the monumental weight of architecture. The atemporal space of the exotic is replaced by a proliferation of historical times.

The search for the exotic had to push on, beyond the frontier of the modernization of the postcolonial and non-metropolitan world. This very process of searching out the exotic exhausts it. Each node of exoticism that is identified, mapped, linked by transport, communication, and infrastructure to the non-exotic world, tends to become, in the process, less and less exotic. What is built, on the ruins of the exotic, is architecture. Architecture, which, while it may incorporate some of the details and features of the exotic, ends up subsuming them within its practice of building.

The exotic only exists when it confronts architecture as a pure, immediate singularity. It is outside the chain of signification. That is its very appeal. The pleasure and danger of the exotic is that it touches the real. In the process of developing from its contact with the exotic, architecture cannot but assimilate it into the chain of signification. Sure, what was there remains different. Not every place has a hotel shaped like a big crocodile, where you enter through its jaws, and check in where its teeth meet. But this is no longer exotic. It's just different.

Gagudju Crocodile Holiday Inn, Australia. Courtesy Holiday Inn

Architecture incorporates the really exotic within the symbolic order, thereby canceling its difference.

These days, both architecture and the exotic, those co-dependent poles, have a common enemy in communication, which tends to cancel out both the historical space of architecture and the atemporal space of the exotic. Since the telegraph detached the flow of information from the movement of people and things, it has been all over for architecture. The very last form of architecture on the planet was the construction of telegraph offices—some of which were very beautiful structures. But they are architecture's mausoleums.

The telegraph, telephone, and television—telesthesia, the communication vector—put core and periphery in touch with each other, at the latter's expense. Globalization begins in earnest with the telegraph. All of space becomes potentially a space of communication, an interior space. The historical space and the exotic space are in immediate contact. The former dominates the latter, while the exotic infiltrates and dissimulates. It yields up its pure otherness to the play of signs.

The telegraph is also the beginning of the age of tourism. There is no tourism without the telegraph, only travel. Tourism, aided and abetted by the telegraph, is the great extinguisher of the exotic. Of course, cultured types abhor the idea of tourism.

More than a thousand couples renew their wedding vows at sea aboard the *Grand Princess,* the largest cruise ship in the world, while en route to St. Thomas for a seven-day Caribbean cruise, 1999. Photo: Tim Chapman, AP Photo

They think they are still travelers, but really they are just different kinds of tourists. Only the homeless are travelers. Only the homeless depart without a destination.

The whole point of tourism used to be that travel was an experience of something other than the home world to which one was otherwise permanently tied. The architecture of tourism was then the antithesis of the norm. It was everything that was expelled from the mundane world, a landscape of fantasy and splendor. Tourism was the means by which a people could take a safe step or two outside the bounded space that formed a home world. A people could step into the exotic world of some other people—or, at least, into an image of this other maintained for this very purpose. One toured, on occasion, to maintain this relation between a people and its other.

Yet these are times when movement has become the norm. The boundaries defining a home world become porous, ambiguous. In place of a people bounded in space and bordered by an other, we find ourselves among a multitude, a heterogeneous continuum that constantly escapes from the identity of a people with its home. More and more this multitude is on the move, sometimes by choice, often not.

One of the signs of the subtle transformation of peoples into multitudes is that what was once the architecture of tourism has become the norm. All architecture is now tourist architecture. Hotels look like condos, and condos like hotels. Malls dabble in the signs of the exotic, while formerly exotic locales become malls. All the tracks are beaten to within an inch of their lives.

To think further about this architecture of the departure lounge, we can turn to Paolo Virno's *Grammar of the Multitude,* in which the distinction between a people and a multitude is given a particularly clear expression. Virno contrasts Hobbes's people, sheltering within the bounds of the state, with Spinoza's multitude, refusing to converge into any kind of unity or stay within any bounds.

The multitude is something that the Hobbesian

aspect of the contemporary state fears and represses. It is, among other things, the relentless flow of refugees, "boat people," and transmigrants, seeping though the pores of the state and its territories. The state finds it troubling even within its borders. Here the multitude employs what Michel de Certeau calls the tactics of everyday life, always avoiding and evading surveillance and control.

In liberal thought, the quirky, proliferating differences of the multitude are relegated to the sphere of the private. The public aspect of the citizen is a universal attribute, something amenable to unification. The private is the remainder. Difference is all right as long as it remains private. But just as communication undoes the gap between architecture and the exotic, so too it undoes the gap between public and private.

Nowhere is the breakdown of the distinction between public and private more evident than in the way the multitude organizes itself with its constant cell-phone calls, blithely talking, in earshot of anyone, about the most personal problems. With the cell phone, the multitude finds its tool for creating its own spatiality, inserting its differences into public space, refusing to keep the details private.

The multitude refuses the ready-made unity of state and nation. It prefers wandering out of bounds, and composes its own open-ended wholeness, one encounter at a time. No wonder states have discovered a newfound fear of it. The obsessive rituals of security checks at airports are the symptom of a state apparatus that finds itself bypassed at every turn by a multitude in motion, on which it yet comes increasingly to depend.

The multitude refuses the separation of public and private, and has no use for the separation of work from leisure. Its work is increasingly a matter of the management of immaterial codes and connections. This is the case not just with the "cognitariat," who trade in signs, but also of the less lucky transmigrants, those escaping from failed states. Their working assets are a multitude made of communal and familial ties, stretching across continents.

The new landscape of transit thus has many classes and comfort levels. You might be sipping piña coladas by the pool or holed up in a detention center for illegal immigrants, but either way it's the same landscape of holding pens seeking to capture, by force or by seduction, an itinerant multitude with no interest in staying put.

The multitude refuses the arbitrary alienation of one aspect of its being from another: work from leisure, private from public. It also refuses more than a temporary capture of its interests in any one place, in any one use of its time. Paolo Virno notes, "The many, in as much as they are many, are those who share the feeling of not feeling at home."[1] Or, as an old Gang of Four song puts it: "At home he feels like a tourist."[2] And on tour she feels perfectly at home.

The multitude comes into its own when it acquires the tools and techniques for making space habitable on its own terms. Its architecture is wireless hotspots, corner stores selling prepaid cell-phone cards, the laundromat with Internet access, the café with last week's newspapers in your mother tongue. Wherever the multitude is in motion, someone will find a way to capture some value from it as it flows by.

Marx, writing about labor in the colonies in *Capital*, already discovers the multitude in motion. "So long, therefore, as the laborer can accumulate for himself—and this he can do so long as he remains possessor of his means of production—capitalist accumulation and the capitalistic mode of production are impossible."[3] So long as labor can find a line along which to escape, and find the resources to realize its own value, it avoids becoming subsumed within capital. In the old world, one aspect of the emergent working class digs in, creates unions and political parties, transforming the liberal into the social state. The other aspect takes the first boat to the New World. It might work for a while in the factories there, but it wants nothing but to take off again, try its luck at prospecting, or maybe open a bar. It escapes from the prospect of being a people to become a multitude.

Hundreds of ethnic Albanian refugees from Kosovo arrive aboard trucks in the northern Albanian town of Kukes, 1999. Photo: Hektor Pustina, AP Photo

To this day the movement of the multitude creates and recreates a building without qualities. It is all over for the architecture of the state and its people. Go to any old mill town in the northeastern United States and you will most likely find a boarded-up main street with a grand police station and a court house facing each other, and a lawyer's office or two, surrounded by nothing. Everybody took off for somewhere else. Maybe the multitude is in a trailer park now, or some instant suburb—the kind architects hate, but that have the virtue of pure impermanence. The multitude isn't kidding itself about stability and propriety. It has given up on civilizing capital, and has decided to try the opposite tack—being even more feral than capital itself.

All building is temporary now, and knows it. It's all box stores and strip malls, office parks and prefab "developments," each replacing the next like slash-and-burn agriculture. One can celebrate it as the new suburban anchor *à la* David Brooks, or condemn it as the soulless blighted world of the "middle mind" *à la* Curtis White.[4] But what's usually lacking is an understanding of the multitude's growing tactical

competence. It no longer expects to settle down.

Architecture and communication have always been two aspects of the same phenomenon. Architecture is communication through time using space; communication is architecture through space using time. What is characteristic of our time is the reversal of priority between them. After a long struggle, communication now trumps architecture. The time-binding techniques of built form are now subordinated to the space-binding techniques of the communication vector. With this reversal comes the rise of the multitude, which uses its competence in communication to escape from the enclosures and spatialized alienations of architecture.

If the state is at a loss for how to capture and stabilize the restless flux of the multitude, capital is on the case. But as I argue elsewhere, perhaps the ruling class is no longer exactly capitalist.[5] The factories and forges are now in the underdeveloped world, and ownership of the means of production is increasingly subordinated to the ownership of the patents, trademarks, and copyrights—"intellectual property"—that governs all production. As the "overdeveloped" world is hollowed out and its working class cast on the scrapheap, the new ruling class cares less and less about its care and feeding. "Welfare reform" is the first step toward abandoning the state's responsibilities to its people, now that its people need no longer be stabilized and managed as a working class.

While the new ruling class abandons its responsibilities to the working class, setting it loose as a dispossessed multitude, it cares more and more for quite another aspect of the multitude—its ability to generate what Jean Baudrillard used to call "sign value."[6] It needs the restless productivity of the multitude to constantly create and recreate the language of desire—a language that it can capture and use as the attractive wrappings for the commodities it has made by the old capitalist method in the underdeveloped world.

The whole of the overdeveloped world becomes a new kind of factory for the production of signs of

value and value for signs. New York, London, Paris, Los Angeles—each is a giant shop floor for making art, cinema, fashion, fiction, or philosophy. Each attracts a new kind of tourist, one who works for the privilege of seeing its sights. They come in the thousands, to be interns or office assistants, turning whole city blocks into hotels, rented by the month or year rather than the night.

All of the separations that once held—between architecture and the exotic, between public and private, between work and leisure—are in each case effaced by the same development, the coming into being of the communication vector. It reorganizes space according to its own lights. Where once the portal was subordinated to the wall, now it is entirely the other way around. Space loses its qualities. Everyday life is determined by tempos of movement and relation.

This is hardly a utopian scenario, however. One tension remains, even if in a new form—the class tension of ownership and dispossession. On the one side, capital mutates, freeing itself from the ownership of things and fetishizing the control of information. All that is solid finally melts into digital bits. On the other side, a multitude comes into being, which overcomes the separation of public and private, work and leisure, and which adds incessant movement to its arsenal of strategies. The struggle for the future moves to a new terrain, leaving behind it, as a charming residue, what was once architecture.

NOTES

1. Paolo Virno, *The Grammar of the Multitude* (New York: Semiotext(e), 1994), 35.

2. Gang of Four, *Entertainment!*, Warner Bros., 1979.

3. Karl Marx, *Capital*, vol. 1, chap. 33, http://www.marxists.org/archive/marx/works/1867-c1/

4. See David Brooks, *On Paradise Drive* (New York: Simon & Schuster, 2004); and Curtis White, *The Middle Mind* (San Francisco: Harper, 2003).

5. See McKenzie Wark, *A Hacker Manifesto* (Cambridge, Mass.: Harvard University Press, 2004).

6. See Jean Baudrillard, *For a Critique of the Political Economy of the Sign* (St. Louis, Mo.: Telos Press, 1981).

TIM EDENSOR
THEATER OF THE EXOTIC: TOURIST SPACE AS STAGE AND PERFORMANCE

As an increasing range of cultural particularities is peddled in the global supermarket, a key marker of difference, the exotic, has become progressively redistributed so that its forms are multiple and hybrid. This expansion has extended the array of "exotic" ethnicities, places, and forms characterized by difference on sale and on display, and yet the exotic remains tethered to those consistent themes that emerged under colonial conditions, an imagined, alluring non-Western alterity embodied in styles of clothing, music, dance, art, architecture, and food.

Situated in store window displays, art galleries, and films, the exotic also persists in certain carnivalesque spaces, from the lurid art of fairgrounds to the simulated, mediatized exotica of malls and theme parks. In architectural style, particular buildings like Brighton Pavilion (in the case of Great Britain) as well as early modern movie palaces reveal the longstanding association of the exotic with pleasure, and numerous, more mundane sites, such as themed restaurants and bars, now supplement these spectacular effusions of oriental fantasy. For instance, in my hometown of Manchester, a restaurant called Persia offers "authentic" dishes together with hubble-bubble pipes, live Persian music, and a luxurious decor that includes plush sofas and drapes. Spaces of this kind promise a transcendent and enthralling otherness but instead are sites where merely a "controlled decontrol of the emotions safely takes place," in the words of social theorist Mike Featherstone.[1] This is accomplished by carefully contextualizing the exotic as a commodity,

precious artifact, or desirable destination, so that its alterity is domesticated and commodified, rendering it unambiguous and epistemologically secure. Such strategies continue to exemplify the fear/desire nexus through which the West has consumed and fantasized about otherness, but it may also fuel a yearning to go beyond this incorporation, to seek out and experience a less containable difference.

Nowhere is the commodification and quest for the exotic more apparent than in tourism. Typically organized around the capture of familiar, famous sights, undisturbed and seamless forms of mobility, and the dissemination of digestible, prepackaged information and reified discourses about places and cultures, tourism emphasizes a series of "appropriate" activities centered on consumption, and regularized itineraries that sew together various attractions. Accordingly, in tourism, the exotic inheres in "timeless" traditions, sensual modes of living, lavishly garbed bodies, lush tropicality, customs and folk displays,

material opulence, and architectural extravaganzas.

Staged and performed tourism is thus a coproduction between tourist personnel and tourists, which frequently reproduces ideas of the exotic.[2] As is evident in some of the examples provided above, the peddling of the exotic has long been suffused by the theatrical effects of particular architectural and design forms, tourist stage sets that are the venue for a battery of techniques and technologies, including audiovisual displays, dramatic reenactments, interactive events in which lighthearted role-playing is expected of tourists, and presentations of folk music and dance.

Equally important to the production of the exotic, however, is the complicity of tourists in performing conventions that simultaneously reproduce the norms of tourism and the meanings of space. Culturally coded patterns of tourist behavior are grounded in a specific, "common-sense," unreflexive *habitus*, following Pierre Bourdieu,[3] and follow shared understandings about what should be enacted and what is inappropriate in particular forms of tourist space. Not only are these habitual performances subject to self-monitoring, but they are also checked to ensure competence by other tourists and further regulated by the "soft control" mobilized by guards, guides, and closed-circuit television cameras.[4] As explained by Jonas Frykman and and Orvar Löfgren, "cultural community is often established by people together tackling the world around them with familiar maneuvers,"[5] a conception that insists that tourism is not an extraordinary but an ordinary activity. Replete with these routinized habits, tourism is increasingly a part of contemporary everyday worlds in which commercial and leisure spaces contain a proliferating range of stages, activities, and identities. These normative enactions do not only produce rigid conventions, however, for they are apt to constitute an identifiable code against which to react. Moreover, given their commonplace character, there is, as Paul Harrison puts it, "always immanent potential for new possibilities of life" in their very mundanity.[6] Accordingly, such conventions and theatrical management cannot wholly determine the kinds of performance that occur and can gesture toward transcendent possibilities.

Although, as Frykman and Löfgren assert, we dwell within "a mobile culture where people constantly meet otherness,"[7] many tourist spaces are organized to secure meaning and performance. Included among these carefully managed, continually reproduced stages are what I have termed "enclavic," single-purpose tourist spaces, arranged to facilitate smooth transit, containing discretely situated props, and marked off from surrounding space by fences and guards. Such spaces contrast with the blurred boundaries, numerous other actors, shifting scenes, and random events or juxtapositions of "heterogeneous" tourist spaces,[8] which conversely are weakly classified, multipurpose spaces.

Sugar Beach Resort, Mauritius. Photo: Tim Edensor

The serial, enclavic spaces of tourism, enmeshed within rigid itineraries, are organized and designed to facilitate the normative enactions of tourists and the dramatic production of theatrical events performed for tourists. Directors and stagehands manage space, and scriptwriters and choreographers—tour guides—negotiate the ways in which tourists act in space, ensuring that conventions of "appropriate," movement, "orderly" behavior, and collective endeavor are followed. There are, moreover, a host of familiar props and fixtures—staircases, café tables, swimming pools, pathways, and balconies—whose smooth textures and uncluttered surrounds mean that seamless movement and a sense of dwelling are not disrupted. The comfortable pleasures of immersion in such spaces, a slowed-down pace of living within a temporary *communitas*, is often subject to critical scrutiny but is paradigmatic of the temporary, intense absorption in highly rationalized and regulated spaces that characterizes many contemporary modes of leisure and social association.[9] The pleasures of reliable and relaxing comfort should not be dismissed. It is only when such spaces proliferate so as to constitute the realm of nearly all leisure experience that they threaten to stifle other, more contingent or expressive forms of leisure.

Exemplifying the touristic staging and performing of the exotic is the Sugar Beach Resort in Mauritius, an upmarket beach resort hotel that accommodates more than five hundred guests. Here, a peculiarly hybridized version of the exotic is architecturally materialized and dramatically performed. Situated in the Indian Ocean, Mauritius was formerly a French colony that owed its prosperity to sugar plantations. Around twenty of these estates remain, operated by the heirs of the original French colonists. The descendants of the Madagascan and East African slaves who were imported to work the plantations now form about 30 percent of the island's variegated ethnic mix. Yet despite the brutal and degrading history inherent in a slave economy, Sugar Beach has adopted a theme that startlingly exoticizes this colonial past.

Like most hotels in Mauritius, Sugar Beach is clearly separated from the local environment by its long driveway, high walls, manicured gardens, and policed boundaries.[10] This enclave provides Western visitors with a recognizable and familiar home away from home within an exotic context, conveyed through gestures inside the resort, but controlled by sheltering tourists from the disorienting effects that may result from too-close contact with "local" space and culture. In order to distinguish itself from the numerous exclusive and upmarket hotels dotted around the Mauritian coast, Sugar Beach promotes a unique theme based on its former plantation economy.

The architectural design of the resort accords with the conventions of the plantation estate and includes extensive palm-studded lawns and swimming pool areas, paintings and sculptures, a restaurant and bar constructed in the colonial style of a sugar mill, a series of villas bearing the name of an actually existing sugar estate, and, most dramatically, a large Manor House containing further accommodations.

The Manor House serves as the venue for a drama staged to welcome new guests to the hotel. The sweeping stairway descending from the large drawing room on the second floor of the building is the stage down which two figures dressed in periwigs and late-nineteenth-century French aristocratic attire descend to the accompaniment of a "colonial" overture composed for the occasion. These two costumed figures—the "marquis" and "marquess" of the estate—gaze upon an equally glamorous couple, a bride and groom, who follow them down the staircase, and these actors are in turn followed by five maids and five waiters who perform graceful, choreographed maneuvers with feather dusters and brooms. The playlet finishes with the resort's manager welcoming the guests and declaring that they are going to enjoy a vacation experience in true colonial style. While these eye-catching staff members are of the appropriate ethnicity for historical verisimilitude, the two couples are not the white Franco-Mauritians they ought to be, but are Creoles. This convolution aside, the inference is clear that the standards of

service offered can be expected to match those of an imaginary colonial era, and the guests are accordingly positioned as the recipients of this service.

At Sugar Beach, Mauritian colonialism is presented as having been a rather benign force instead of the brutally iniquitous regime it undoubtedly was. Yet this romantic staging is a hybrid exoticism, a globally informed production that besides historical citations simultaneously references glitzy fashion, the historical costume dramas of film and television ranging from *Gone with the Wind* to *Pride and Prejudice,* and other broad allusions to the "grace" of colonial living, the erotics of the colonial master-servant relationship, and the broad allure of a tropical paradise.

The resort has been designed as a space for the performance of exoticism, a staging that requires visitors to be complicit in this performance, to also play their part in this colonial atmosphere as honored guests who will receive fastidious and indulgent treatment from the staff. Themed spaces like this are designed to foster normative performances from tourists while provoking imaginative improvisations and sensations that resonate with the theme being offered. Like other resorts, Sugar Beach is a smooth space, replete with certain designed signifiers of a colonial exotic, an ensemble of specific affordances that stimulate imaginative "colonial" enactions, including the carefully planted palm trees swaying in the breeze, the comfortable cane chairs, the piped-in music, the textures of pavements and lawns, the sweeping stairways, fixtures, and textures that

Sugar Beach Resort, Mauritius. Photo: Tim Edensor

suggest styles of walking, the swish of gown upon floor, and the chink of glasses in the evening. This is a stage whose design and materiality cajoles tourists into specific kinds of performances, making them complicit in the production of themed space. The production of romantic, exotic colonialism depends on a careful design—one that blends media references, staged shows, contextualized artifacts, and historical allusions that minimize the cold-hearted reality of colonialism and meld the materialized theme so that it accords with the imperative to reproduce the conventions of this kind of tourist space and performance.

Is there an alternative to the production of this customized exoticism achieved through the iteration of touristic performative conventions and the provision of dramatic stagings upon theatrical spaces? Such productions depend on the desire to confront difference, to transcend the everyday, and yet this is all too likely to result in realms of controlled disorder, in which tourist performance sidesteps dialogue, improvisation, and conjecture in the confrontation in favor of a highly coded, contained difference.[11] To provide a contrast with the production of such themed tourist spaces and their coproduction through the complicit enactions performed by tourists, I offer the radically alternative space of the industrial ruin.

In the British industrial ruins to which I am drawn, a different kind of spatial aesthetic dominates, and an alternative performative disposition is required.[12] There are no guides to direct performance and no fellow tourists to monitor the limits of appropriate enaction. Such ruins provide the opportunity to encounter difference, yet this is an alterity that cannot be clearly framed, contextualized, or commodified. There is nothing to buy and nothing conforms to the staged aesthetics of tourist space. These kinds of ruins thwart the quest for a comfortable encounter with the exotic and are never referred to in media or tourist guidebooks, requiring visitors to compose their own pathways.

As a stage, the ruin is not managed but is the result of the arbitrary happenstance of decay. While ruins

contain a profusion of props around which performance might occur, these props may be dangerous (as in the case of a rickety staircase), possess an obscurity of purpose, lack the smooth and comfortable textures of the carefully maintained, or even a clear discreteness, as they decay and merge with other objects and life forms. Obsolete machines used for obscure industrial procedures provoke imaginative interpretation, while other unexpected sights and objects are unfathomable, peculiar sculptures and strange juxtapositions chanced upon. With matter scattered and distributed in a seemingly arbitrary fashion, there are no preparations for entry into, and performance upon, such a stage; and these scenes do not allow smooth and sequential movement around preferred pathways, for multiple routes may be followed. Movement is rough, persistently disrupted, and potentially perilous, replete with sensations other than those experienced through a distanced gaze. The lack of obvious spectacles around which the sensual apprehension of space might be organized is replaced by a multisensual encounter with disordered space. Unfamiliar smells, sounds, and textures impose themselves upon the body, decentering the visual and foregrounding an immanent awareness of the uncommon materialities that contrast with the largely sensually ordered world outside, and in the regulated tourist enclaves discussed above. The body's sensory faculties are provoked, and the interpenetration of the outside and inside through the invasion of smells, dust, and sounds produce a performance that is the antithesis of the stately touristic progress through enclavic stages.[13] The lack of any rehearsed or scripted roles means that the visitor to a ruin must adopt an improvisatory disposition.

Yet rather than being devoid of performative resonances, the scenes of disorder, the uncanny relationships between things, and the weird positioning of objects have a propensity to suggest the aftermath of mysterious dramas; such scenes might be the traces of unfathomable acts between unknowable agents. This reinforces the way in which encountering ruined space leads to a failure to fix meaning or enact conventional routines in space. Instead, such travels open up possibilities for imagination, for conjecture and an acceptance that what is experienced can be pleasurably indeterminate. Rather than the commodified and carefully contextualized features of the exotic—its glamorized history and its cast of recognizable others—in the ruin there are only ghostly traces with which to conjure, partial and incomprehensible scripts undergoing decay,[14] and illegible, technical language belonging to a spectral cast. In the ruin, the ambiguities that inhere in all space are especially apparent. Unlike the increasingly themed, staged, aestheticized, disciplined, highly regulated, smooth, homogeneous, and interconnected spaces of organized tourism, the experience of the ruin cannot be inserted into a prearranged vocabulary in which it is classified as exotic. In encountering the ruin there is, nevertheless, a pervasive sense of otherness and difference—but one that is intangible and slippery.

NOTES

1. Mike Featherstone, *Consumer Culture and Postmodernism* (London: Sage, 1991), 78.

2. Tim Edensor, "Performing Tourism, Staging Tourism: (Re)Producing Tourist Space and Practice," *Tourist Studies* 1 (2001): 59–82.

3. Pierre Bourdieu, *Distinction: A Social Critique of the Judgment of Taste*, translated by Richard Nice (Cambridge, Mass.: Harvard University Press, 1984).

4. George Ritzer and Allen Liska, "'McDisneyization' and 'Post-Tourism': Complementary Perspectives on Contemporary Tourism," in *Touring Cultures: Transformations of Travel and Theory*, edited by Chris Rojek and John Urry (New York and London: Routledge, 1997), 106.

5. Jonas Frykman and Orvar Löfgren, eds., Introduction, *Forces of Habit: Exploring Everyday Culture* (Lund, Sweden: Lund University Press, 1996), 10–11.

6. Paul Harrison, "Making Sense: Embodiment and the Sensibilities of the Everyday," *Environment and Planning D: Society and Space* 18 (2000): 498.

7. Frykman and Löfgren, eds., Introduction, *Forces of Habit*, 14.

8. Tim Edensor, *Tourists at the Taj: Performance and Meaning at a Symbolic Site* (London: Routledge, 1998).

9. Michel Maffesoli, *The Time of the Tribes: The Decline of Individualism in Mass Society,* translated by Don Smith (London: Sage, 1996).

10. Tim Edensor and Uma Kothari, "Sweetening Colonialism: A Mauritian Themed Resort," in D. Medina Lasansky and Brian McClaren, eds., *Architecture and Tourism* (Oxford: Berg, 2004), 185–205.

11. Claudio Minca and Tim Oakes, eds., Introduction, *Tourism and the Paradox of Modernity* (Minneapolis: University of Minnesota Press, 2005).

12. Tim Edensor, *Industrial Ruins: Space, Aesthetics and Materiality* (Oxford: Berg, 2005).

13. Tim Edensor, "Sensing Tourist Spaces," in Minca and Oakes, eds., *Tourism and the Paradox of Modernity.*

14 Tim Edensor, "The Ghosts of Industrial Ruins: Ordering and Disordering Memory in Excessive Space," *Environment and Planning D: Society and Space* (2005).

DETOUR
WEST KOWLOON, HONG KONG

A centerpiece project of the first administration to take office in Hong Kong after the city returned to Chinese rule in 1997, West Kowloon Cultural District was envisioned as a vehicle for making the city the arts hub of twenty-first-century Asia. The site, comprising some 98 acres of reclaimed harborfront land, was slated to house a mixed-use culture and leisure zone including world-class museums and performance venues. An international juried competition for a "concept plan" was held under Hong Kong's then chief executive, Tung Chee-Hwa. Among its criteria was that the proposal establish a unique architectural landmark.

The winning scheme, announced in 2002, was by the British architect Norman Foster, already well known in Hong Kong for his high-tech headquarters for the Hong Kong and Shanghai Bank and Chep Lap Kok Airport. Foster's plan features a giant undulating clear plastic canopy sheltering at least four theaters, a sports stadium, museums, galleries, art schools and studios, as well as an open-air plaza and park, and retail and residential spaces. The jury acknowledged the canopy's potential to create visual coherence and serve as a tourist icon for the new Hong Kong. The plan also includes a continuous promenade that follows the curves of the waterfront. Rather than compete with the skyscrapers beyond the site, the horizontal scheme allows Hong Kong's tall buildings to form a dramatic backdrop.

Foster's plan became the subject of public controversy almost immediately. The multi-billion-dollar price tag was deemed too expensive, and the canopy, touted as providing a controlled microclimate permitting all-weather activity and recalling (in warped form) Buckminster Fuller's visionary project of 1960 for a gigantic dome over midtown Manhattan, was termed impractical by engineers and even other architects. Critics feared it would have a humid greenhouse effect and be vulnerable to typhoons. But strongest opposition was aroused by the government's intent to award development rights to a single large consortium, calling forth accusations that the project was a product of collusion between big government and big business. A protest demonstration took place on Christmas Day in 2004 and drew hundreds of participants. Tung resigned under pressure in early 2005, leaving West Kowloon in limbo.

As of spring 2005, while the Chinese government and the city's new leader, Donald Tsang, have affirmed their determination to go forward and have defended Foster's project, it remains unclear how much will ultimately be built. Meanwhile proposals for individual institutions within the district have been solicited, with the Guggenheim Museum and the Pompidou Center among those vying to create lucrative Asian outposts under Foster's big canopy.

WEST KOWLOON CULTURAL DISTRICT

ACKBAR ABBAS
EXOTIC WITH AN "X"

Since June 1997, when Hong Kong reverted to Chinese rule, this former British colony has seen a dwindling number of visitors from Japan—once the mainstay of its tourist industry. One intriguing reason given for this state of affairs, in addition to the economic crisis that has hampered Asia since the late 1990s, is that because Hong Kong is no longer British, it is less foreign and hence less exotic to its Japanese neighbors. The city in general remains unchanged: the airport is still the best airport in the world; the buildings by Norman Foster, I. M. Pei, and a host of other international architects still stand; it is still a great place to shop. On one level, the picture has not changed at all; what has changed is that it is now framed for Japan as more "Asian" than "foreign" and too close to home to be exotic.

The example of Hong Kong suggests some familiar thoughts and perhaps some new questions in relation to the notion of the exotic. The first idea is that exoticism is not an objective quality of places, but a subjective response to them. It is not a fact, but an effect: the effect of otherness that certain places have on us. At the same time, the case of Hong Kong demonstrates that the exotic as an effect of otherness is highly unstable and fickle; it evaporates for the most preposterous of reasons. This suggests that the exotic never offered real otherness to begin with, but only clichés of otherness, which are easier to both adopt and discard. If one brings in the argument that globalism has meant the disappearance of distance and differentiation, the exotic no longer becomes an

encounter with the strange, the unknown, or the different, but rather an attempt at synthesizing or faking these vanished qualities of places. Today's exotic, according to this argument, stresses differences that do not make a difference, strangeness that does not produce estrangement or puzzlement, and an "unknown" that does not challenge or upset one's sense of the known. As a form of relation to otherness, the exotic, it seems, is tolerant to a fault.

This is not the whole story, however, and it is possible and even important to try to imagine the exotic taking on new forms and functions in the global age. First, it is not essential to think of the exotic as the distant and unfamiliar. It could very well be the close at hand and elusive, comparable to the

way in which colonialism is both close at hand and elusive: where we think it to be, it is not, and where we do not expect it, we find it still. In this aspect, a comparison of Hong Kong before and after mid–1997 offers an especially illuminating case study of both the exotic and the colonial. Colonialism as it existed before the British mandate ended there seemed to bear little resemblance to what is commonly critiqued in textbooks. There was, on one hand, Hong Kong's ambiguous relationship with China; and on the other hand, the gradual morphing of an imperialist model into a globalist paradigm—one that even took on benign-looking characteristics. This is neither colonialism nor postcolonialism, but rather "X"-colonialism. There is an "X" too in the exotic, and as in the X-colonial, the X suggests not just the

unknown but more precisely the figure of chiasmus, a critical point of crossover. The exotic then exists and persists in a whole series of mundane migrancies that make the familiar elusive, occupying a gray area marked not by violent displacements but by small dislocations. Its cultural politics is the politics of the detail. This leads to another important way of thinking about the exotic, namely, not in terms of how one place is different from another, but in terms of how a place is different or distanced from itself. The exotic, that is, is not just an elsewhere; it is

A tricycle rider delivers computer monitors in Zhongguancun, a modern three-mile-long street that has become Beijing's answer to Silicon Valley, 1999. Photo: Greg Baker, AP Photo

always elsewhere, even when close at hand. The spaces it evokes are spaces that slip away if we try to grasp them too definitively or too literally.

These ruminations on the exotic and its ambivalences have a certain bearing on the concept of architourism, an idea that is also not without its ambivalences. For most tourists in urban areas, not to mention architects themselves, architecture provides the first quick visual fix on a place being visited, as buildings are usually the largest and most visible images of a city. Like Wallace Stevens's jar in Tennessee, they take dominion everywhere. But images of the city, like city logos, now tell us very little about a city. We have only to note that no matter in which part of the world, whether it is Potsdamerplatz or Pudong—whenever architecture is built from a tabula rasa—it seems to show a penchant for a universal language of spectacle and the exoticism of the new. It therefore might be useful to draw on another understanding of the exotic at this point, and to ask in what ways specific examples of architecture are elusive and other to the city itself. This is also a way of asking how the exotic intervenes in the cultural politics of global tourism.

To explore this further, one may look at three Chinese cities in particular—Shanghai, Beijing, as well as Hong Kong—all popular tourist destinations that have been transformed by new architecture. This is something that every tourist notices, in fact, cannot help noticing, because new buildings are everywhere; so that whether or not architecture is the intended destination for tourism, it becomes a focal point. Most tourists soon notice that there is

Herzog & de Meuron, project for the 2008 Olympic Stadium for Beijing, 2003.

something not quite right about these new buildings that appear to try hard to look modern and in effect nondescript; there are either details missing, or too many extraneous details, usually in the form of add-ons that attempt to assert a "Chinese" identity—a form of exoticism.

One kind of tourist will act the part of the latter-day colonialist and dismiss what is built as merely a poor imitation of Western architecture that is not quite there yet. But another kind of tourist—while remaining a tourist without turning into a deconstructive critic—will note in the spatial anomalies and "exotic" details the presence of cultural interference or "noise," and recognize that something historically more complex and paradoxical is taking place. This is the exotic as paradox and fascination, in contrast to the exotic as doxa and clichés of otherness. The exotic as paradox is more noticeable to an outsider—which is by definition what the tourist must be—than to an insider. Walter Benjamin's much maligned "tourist gaze" is a superficial gaze, not a studious one, but that is precisely both its limits and its peculiar advantage. The tourist gaze is a distracted gaze, and distraction, as Benjamin has reminded us, does not necessarily signify a lack of attention; it may signify a different kind of attention, in the form of a "heightened presence of mind." We should neither under- nor overestimate this state of mind. It is interesting too that Benjamin makes the point exactly at the moment when he compares architecture to cinema—specifically, to cinema as an art of movement, which is also what tourism, in a different sense, can be.

Paradox also marks Beijing, the oldest of the three cities mentioned, and the slowest to change. But it is changing now, with China's entry into the World Trade Organization and the capital's designation as the venue for the 2008 Olympic Games. Changan Avenue, which cuts through Tiananmen Square and the Forbidden City as an east-west axis, is a showcase for new architecture, whose aim is to construct an irreproachable image of

a Beijing newly arisen from its dogmatic slumber. It is in the less frequently highlighted parts of the city, the working-class neighborhoods, however, that spatial contradictions are more striking.

For example, on Guanganmen Avenue in southern Beijing, hundreds of *hutongs* (ancient narrow streets) have been demolished. From their ashes has arisen a highway lined on both sides with dozens of four-story malls. There are literally miles and miles of these malls, all new and empty, awaiting occupation by the emergent class of entrepreneurs. The air is full of expectation, but ironically the strongest impression is that of a ghost town. It is, to be sure, a paradoxical kind of ghost town: a new rather than dilapidated ghost town; a ghost town haunted not by the past but by the future.

It is in the nature of the exotic, it seems to me, to be wrapped up in such paradoxes. But then, it is the exotic as paradox that leads the tourist gaze, and the argument about architourism, elsewhere.

MARTHA ROSLER
IN THE PLACE OF THE PUBLIC: AIRPORT SERIES

Ongoing
Color photographs with text

Desire in airports is always infinitely deferred, and meaning is elsewhere and otherwise. Back-lit photos lure us to Tahiti or to Cincinnati (unless we are in Tahiti or Cincinnati), to Disneyland or to the Eiffel Tower, to Marlboro Country or to the land of financial accumulation, telephones, and computers or (alternatively) of remote, outmoded forms of transportation, such as the canoe trip in rural Africa—and sometimes both simultaneously. All are equivalent possibilities for fantasy destinations, all for some reason more interesting than the view awaiting the flyer outside the window.

The frustrating sameness of tourist destinations, while often overstated, nonetheless underscores the fundamental tendency toward the homogenization of culture. The beaten path beats down that which it managed to reach with such difficulty. Erasure of difference always leads to efforts by the global colonizer to "preserve" it, but as a depoliticized, aestheticized set of cultural practices, as a "destination" module.

This sameness blanketing the world to uneven depths (and with however many rents in the fabric) simultaneously reassures and defeats the traveler. The crippling comforts of the advanced world, which appear in many guises in far-flung locales, ensure that the businessman tied to global networks never shucks his bonds. So long as the means to phone home are retained at will, everywhere is anywhere. "The economic organization of visits to different places is already in itself the guarantee of their equivalence. The same modernization that removed the voyage from time also removed it from the reality of space." (Guy Debord, *The Society of the Spectacle*)

heightened docility militant flags photography prohibited specters of dread walls behind walls tweezers, cell phones, laptop

weapons of mass distraction gelid anxieties suspended between dread and desire you are being watched

shoes stoppages and blockages haunted trajectories convulsive anxieties shopping and waiting, shopping and waiting soft

evasive repressions   rumors of pollution hyperpower   state security apparatus   color-coded execrations

interpenetration of terrors   concentrated gazing   total information mining

resignation and compliance

paranoias of betrayal   one-way information flow   imploded fantasies of escape   psychic confusion

MARK ROBBINS
IMPORT / EXPORT

2000–01
12 billboards

A series of billboards was produced in response to the area along the Miami River. Now a somewhat marginal residential and commercial corridor, the site has a rich ethnic history of control, ownership, and succession, from Native American to Hispanic to English back to Hispanic, mirroring the larger history of Miami itself.

The subjects of the billboards were the Haitians, Dominicans, and Salvadorans who work on the ships that ply the shallow-draft port of the river, hauling piles of used mattresses, furniture, cars, and bicycles to the Caribbean and Central America. Group portraits of these immigrant workers were juxtaposed with images of Miami as seen in tourist brochures: the gleaming skyline, a pleasure cruiser berthed in the city's grand port, a baroque gilded interior from the 1920s. The juxtapositions contrasted Miami's contemporary urban realities of economic hardship and rapid social change with its mythology of leisure and wealth.

Like the flow of goods on this working river at the edge of the glossy contemporary city, Miami's most recent immigrants are largely invisible in its social life and economy. The Cuban-American presence—a variation on the dominant image of the Anglo colonial elsewhere—overshadows other emerging as well as more established cultural groups. Commissioned by the Miami Art Project, the billboards were located in the different neighborhoods that flank the Miami River, which are composed of Cuban, African-American, and Anglo residents. They were intended to import these unheralded members of the most recent cycle of colonization, settlement, and assimilation into the expanding Miami community. Evolving between immigration and tourism, Miami is the American condition in overdrive.

PIERO STEINLE
ISLAND

2002
Stills from audiovisual installation, 43 minutes

Contemporary Iceland: wishes, illusions, fictions, fantasies. Wild nature, unspoiled by man—but only for a limited time. In the footsteps of the pioneers and explorers, pursuing adventure, freedom, and open space, come the tourists, their late descendants. It's a romantic trip into the wilderness, but with return guaranteed. A phantasmagoric landscape, but safe and visitable. A *hortus conclusus*.

While Iceland's endless solitary roads terminate in a single, neat house or a lonely church, nearly always surrounded by a simple enclosure marking the boundaries of the site, its recreational inclinations condense in an idyll of public swimming pools, often situated at what seems to be the edge of the civilized world. The violent, volcanic powers are tamed and contained in these omnipresent volumes of water, heated and nourished by hot springs, frequently painted blue and rectangular.

Island explores the interdependence between desires for escape and their incarnation in reality. It's a complicitous double daydream between Iceland's tourists and its native inhabitants. The video, including still and moving images, was filmed in late September, after all the tourists had departed. The island felt like a playground after closing, suddenly abandoned, off limits and out of time. A slightly hallucinatory world, both intensely artificial and intensely real. An island experience, par excellence.

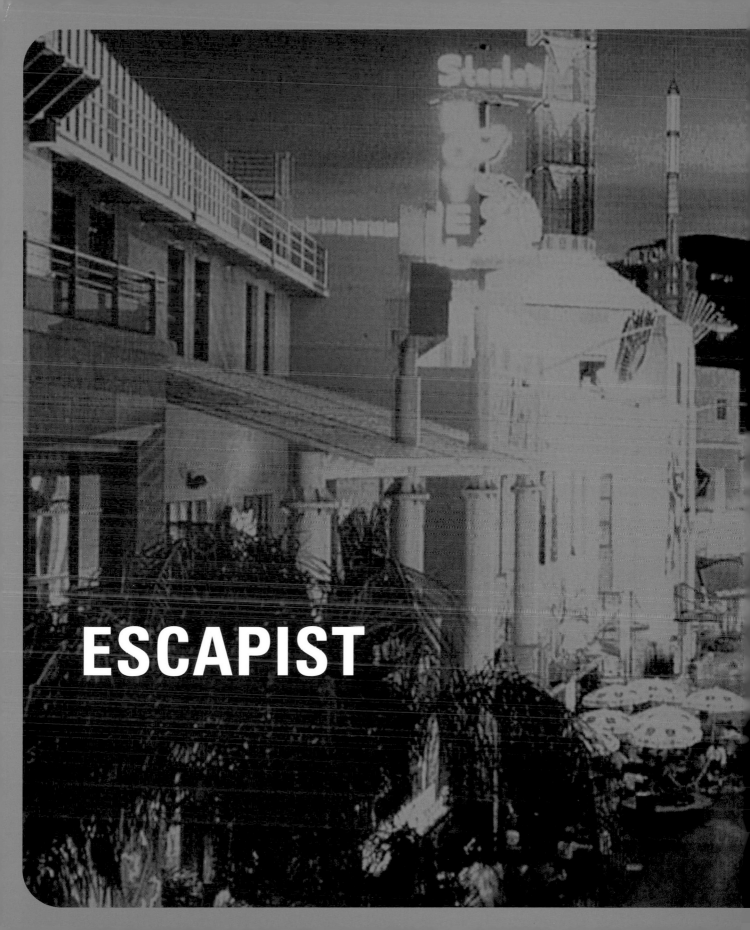

ESCAPIST

Jean Baudrillard has analyzed contemporary culture through the figure of Disneyland, thereby inserting a form of simulated architourism into the heart of his definition of hyperreality. Disneyland is presented as an imaginary kingdom, set aside from the values of everyday America. As such, it serves as a "prop" to make us believe that the world outside is "real." For Baudrillard, however, the world outside is not "real" but "hyperreal," and Disneyland is no different from that world. Disneyland is precisely part of—in fact, a condensation of—the values of America. The corollary, it might be argued, must also be true. If Disneyland is part of America, so too is America part of Disneyland. The logic of role-playing and theming is not limited to Disneyland. It has permeated the whole of America, and indeed the whole of Western society.

We live in a culture of escapist dreaming, fueled by the media. It is as though the only effective strategy for dealing with the *horror vacui* of contemporary existence has become a form of fantasy escapism, based on role-playing and theming. Television soap operas, movies, and pop-music videos, along with consumer magazines, provide us with catalogues of wish-images, which we might incorporate into our lives and on which to model our selves. It is as though we have turned into animated mannequins, acting out our lives according to the well-rehearsed steps of some Hollywood role model.

Advertisements play a crucial role in fostering this cult of the make-believe. They are intended to conjure up in a Proustian manner a whole dreamworld of lifestyling and commodity consumption. Viewers are invited to imagine themselves in the scenario depicted, transported there as though on some magic carpet, and then to retain that fantasy within the "real" world once they have acquired whatever product is being advertised. Nor should we dismiss advertising as an incidental and irrelevant aspect of contemporary life. For advertising, as Andrew Wernick has observed in his book *Promotional Culture,* has so colonized our symbolic horizons that it is all but coextensive with the way in which we see the world these days.

Everyday life is colonized by fantasy. It is dominated by escapist dreaming. This condition pervades the whole of society, not least the domain of architourism. But what this suggests is that architourism is not limited to actual physical tourism. There is no need for physical escapism to actually escape, but so too, physical escapism does not stand outside mental escapism. Journals such as *Wallpaper** offer fantasy escapisms that need not be enacted in a material way, so much as fantasized about within the imagination. Meanwhile our engagement with the material world of architourism is always filtered through an imagination saturated with fantasy and dreaming. It is an imagination, moreover, conditioned by a culture of aestheticization, which operates as a kind of rose-tinted lens, abstracting the world from its harsh material reality, and repackaging it as an anaestheticized version of itself. As such we might recognize that no architecture can escape this condition. Let us therefore acknowledge that both the architourism of "authentic" architectural icons, and the architourism of simulated architectural icons, such as Disneyland or Las Vegas, are inscribed within the same logic of escapist dreaming.

NEIL LEACH

YI-FU TUAN
ARCHITECTURE, ROUTE TO TRANSCENDENCE

Escapism is an ambivalent, even negative word when juxtaposed against *realism* or *authenticity*. Yet insofar as we are sensate beings, we are inescapably escapists. All animals escape when confronted by some sort of threat, when they are pushed. Humans are no different. What makes us different is that we are not only pushed, but are also pulled by some preferred, imagined reality that is either already in existence, "out there," to be discovered, or is a possibility to be realized—that is, constructed.

These constructions may be largely intellectual—for instance, philosophies, religious beliefs, songs, myths, legends, and stories in general; or they may be images and concepts rendered into tangible objects and environments—for instance, tools and artworks, buildings, and towns and cities. Religion, according to some, is escapist; it is something humans have made up to console themselves in the face of the seeming indifference of nature. But, then, we must ask, what is it we make that is not a consolation, not a protection, against the harshness and indifference of both nature and other people?

On a very basic level, I could say that when it rains I escape into a hut that I have made specifically to guard against this and other contingencies. Transforming "nature" into "world," or escaping from the given into the desirable, is what we humans have always done and will surely always want to do. In the past, hunter-gatherers lived in forests that they did not alter to any great degree. It would seem that they were satisfied with the given, that they had no wish to remake it—to escape. Yet this is obviously not true:

our hunter-gatherer ancestors did not live in the midst of nature but rather in a nature that they turned into a significant and reassuring world by means of the stories they told and the dances they performed. People with more powerful tools and skills do not depend solely on images, stories, and dances to create a world. They can also create one materially. Depending on the resources at their command, humans have turned nature into villages and fields, villages into towns, and towns into cities.

This, in capsule form, is the story of human geography. Escapism is a thread that runs through that story. Its various forms in modern times have included—starting with the most obviously escapist— theme parks, shopping malls, and suburban developments. Shopping malls have often been excoriated as a fantasy world of easy fulfillments. In contrast, suburbs, with which malls and consumer emporia are often associated, are real places in the sense that people do not just visit them, but live there. Nevertheless, many well-educated people (academics in particular) have not hesitated to

dismiss them as unreal. Their preference is for the city. To farmers, however, genuine life is not to be found in the showy bustle of the city but rather on the land, close to the soil. Even farmers do not have the last word. The hunter-gatherer societies that still exist today may well consider the tilled fields and farming villages too artifactual, and a little unreal.

A popular automobile bumper sticker observed in the Midwest reads, "Escape to Wisconsin!" The state takes in millions of dollars every year from tourists who seasonally leave densely built Chicago for Wisconsin's relative emptiness. To tourists, this can seem like an escape into nature, as they drive north and see fewer and fewer people and buildings. But, on closer examination, it becomes clear that this is not the case, for two reasons. The first is that even the wildest Wisconsin landscapes have been altered materially, although the alterations may not be visible to the untrained eye. Second, the ways in which tourists experience these landscapes are colored— often unbeknown to themselves—by images and conceptions of nature that are the products of sophisticated urban culture. Escape to Wisconsin is thus not so much escape into nature as escape into culturally generated ideals of nature and the natural. Tourism is always artifactual. What attracts and lures people are either mental images of nature to which nature "out there" is expected to conform, or images and plans that have been turned successfully into artifacts and architecture.

On a grand scale, the city is a shelter akin to the hut that provides shelter from the rain. Humans, at a certain stage in their social evolution, have been drawn to build a place that not only protects them against the vagaries of nature but also has the power to elevate their spirit and make them see themselves as denizens of a harmonious universe rather than merely as creatures that crawl the earth. The earliest cities, according to historians and historical geographers, did not grow out of villages and towns through haphazard processes of accretion; rather, they were—at least originally—ritualized, formal centers, cosmic diagrams conceived and built monumentally

from the start. They testify to the desire to escape the arbitrariness, unpredictability, and constraints of everyday life. Building a city that reflects the orderly motion of the stars, far removed from the hodgepodge of hills and streams, dirt roads, and unkempt villages on earth, is civilization's earliest and most spectacular reach for transcendence.

Once built, however, the heavenly city does not remain pristine for long. Almost immediately, traders, artisans, and skilled and unskilled workers of all sorts move in from the surrounding countryside and beyond. The impressive buildings and associated rituals still stand, of course, but in the minds of most residents they have retreated into the background, displaced by the humbler houses and stores, the myriad economic and social activities that constitute the satisfactions and stresses of daily living. Government officials no doubt retain longer their awareness of the eloquent architectural setting and all that it means; but in time the surroundings can seem oppressive and the ceremonies burdensome. People may then dream of the peace and unpretentiousness of the family farm, and go there when they can to be refreshed and renewed. For both ordinary and elite residents, a pattern of movement between city and countryside is established: those who find shelter and a trade in the city in winter return to work on the farm in summer. The elite move seasonally too, but more for leisure than for work, and their timing is less predictable.

This ebb and flow of populations is a common occurrence in both traditional and modern cities. Whatever we call it, it is not tourism and those who take part in it are not tourists. They—especially the elite in traditional society—do, however, have one thing in common with true tourists. If they move, it is not because of push, but of pull: they are drawn to a place; to the city for its promise of fulfillment of social aspirations—a promise made tangible by magnificent buildings; and to the country for its solitude and closeness to nature.

The widespread practice of tourism, on the other hand, is a modern, middle-class phenomenon. It presupposes a stable and fairly affluent society in

which people have steady jobs, raise their families in good homes, and can count on congenial golf partners on the weekends. Is this life "for real," to use an American colloquialism? It is, to judge by two criteria. One is permanence: people actually live the life over a period of years and longer. The other is stress, not overwhelming stress, but the persistent or low-level stresses related to work, keeping up with one's neighbors, and maintaining the physical condition of one's house and block. A routine of this kind—perhaps routine of any kind—sooner or later makes one ask, Is this all that life is, a low-fever burn and irritation interspersed with mild pleasure that ends in death? Time, then, to escape—take a vacation, be a tourist.

But where? The answer is, any place at a remove from home where chores, even if they exist, are not routine; where watches and cell phones can be left behind; where one's body is reinvigorated and mind enlarged, where, in a euphoric mood, one may even think oneself more than a mortal. It must be emphasized that the place cannot be simply next door, or in cyberspace and available at the tap of a computer key; it must be some distance away such that an effort is needed to reach it, for this effort (travail or travel) can in itself produce the feeling that one is after a real, nontrivial experience, that the place one goes to for renewal has the power to affect one.

As to the character of this place, it can be nature, architecture, or a combination of both. Touring nature, as noted above, is a sophisticated and late development. Historically, in almost all parts of the world, nature is avoided rather than sought after, for, as a matter of common experience, it is the built environment rather than nature that offers not only a life of security and ease, but excitement and novelty as well. Even today, far more people escape to the perceived glamor of cities than to wilderness camps. Of course, the built environment can and, all too often, does repel. Architecture as constructed place is something else.

Thousands crowd St. Peter's Square at the Vatican, looking down Via della Conciliazione, 2000. Photo: Marco Ravagli, AP Photo

Two types of constructed place, among others, that have attracted large numbers of visitors are the theme park and the great building. The most well-known successful theme park offers a magical world that provides almost everything a human being could reasonably want—if not home, then a Main Street that evokes comfort and familiarity, woodlands and rivers, thrill rides and adventures, and glimpses into the future. All these features are, in a sense, not real: they are scaled-down models of realities "out there," but rendered safe and accessible in a such a way that quaint shops selling candy and toys are only a stone's throw away from the hippopotamuses and alligators of Jungle River, and the past of a Mississippi boat ride presses hard against the future of a spin on the Astro Orbiter, a version of which was first envisioned by Leonardo da Vinci five hundred years ago.

Critics, most of them literary academics, consider the Disney theme parks fakes, a sort of deception, an invitation to fantasy and daydreaming that is not in the least educational. Yet if illustrated geography books, capsule histories, legends, and fairy tales are good for young people, why are three-dimensional models of them, many ingeniously constructed, not good? Why is an impressively sized model of the Matterhorn considered escapist and inauthentic, but a painting or photograph of it not viewed this way? Can it be that whereas even children do not mistake a story or a painting for reality, they just may see the safe, miniaturized worlds of Disneyland as real and so be lured into a false sense of not only security but size and scale? Where, in Disneyland, is the sweeping view, space reaching to distant horizons, that invites creative daydreaming?

In contrast, the second popular tourist attraction, the great building, is not a copy or model of any preexistent reality, unless it is that of the cosmos, understood as the perfection of space and splendor, a religious concept that guided the building of the world's major churches and temples. In our increasingly secular age, the sense of spiritual escape can be extended to include the spaces of a magnificent piece of architecture, however it is used,

as a house of God or a house of Art—Chartres Cathedral or the Guggenheim Museum in Bilbao. Visitors may describe their experience in either building as only sensory, but the feast of the senses is such that it rises to, and is hardly distinguishable from, the spiritual. That merging of the sensory with the spiritual is somewhat mysterious. Even the impression of size in the interior vaulting of buildings is imperfectly understood, for, in actual fact, space enclosed by even the largest building is small compared with nature's enclosed spaces, for instance, a river basin or valley. Yet it is the interior of a building—say, Saint Peter's basilica—and not the much larger space of a basin or valley that produces a powerful sensation of size and exaltation.

Any change in life's direction can be a release. Hence, almost any place—even an ordinary farm or an old homestead—can be a destination for tourists. Nevertheless, release is greatest and can have a lingering effect when the change is from the mundane to the transcendent, from a life that answers our basic biological needs to a life that appeals to the mind and spirit. This shift in orientation can occur when we expose ourselves to literature, painting, or music, but only if we have prepared the ground with previous learning and only if we exert ourselves. Even nature, to have a powerful effect on our orientation, requires previous study and knowledge, though an exception may be made of nature that takes the clean architectural form of a stone bridge, a Monument Valley, or a Grand Canyon.

And by architectural, I mean the works of great architects. As with Monument Valley or the Grand Canyon, visitors to a magnificent building can be lifted out of the mundane to the transcendent by just entering it, without detailed knowledge of who built it, when it was built, or how it was built. It is this accessibility—this offering of immediate sensorial and ultrasensorial rewards—that makes architecture different from the literary arts and music. Is it any wonder, then, that architecture, the easiest route of escape to the transcendent, attracts such huge crowds of tourists?

KARAL ANN MARLING
ESCAPISM?

The term "escapism" is often used to mean avoidance; yet it can be regarded instead as an occasion for a transformation, a dislocation, and ultimately, as Yi-Fu Tuan has described it, a kind of transcendence. The Christmas season in America provides such an occasion. A good example is the Christmas tree that is put up every year in New York City's Rockefeller Center—one of the great verticals, according to Tuan. It interrupts the normality of the cityscape just as Christmas interrupts the ebb and flow of a normal year. The tree is a fantasy: big, electric, bumptious—the characteristics of many tourist sites. Such sites are occasions for the creation of fantasies.

Within the realm of one's own home, the Christmas tree has much the same function. In addition to serving as an opportunity for the display of our everyday aesthetic sensibilities, the decorated tree marks a point at which the usual workaday house is transformed into something like a religious shrine—a family shrine. In these circumstances, too, the vernacular architecture of the home becomes something new and different, and certainly unlike what the designer or the builder had in mind.

Similar is the case of the business or civic entity that disguises itself by night during the Christmas season as something other than what it ordinarily is. From the 1940s through the 1960s, long lines of family cars snaked through festively lighted downtowns in most American cities to see window displays, animated figures, and twinkling lights. A store is just a store for eleven months out of the year. But at Christmastime, ablaze with colored lights, the store, the factory, and the city hall comprise a spectacle that transforms both the environment around it and those who go to see it.

Then there are the Christmas villages, which suggest a different kind of transformation. These consist of little stores, houses, and churches made of ceramic materials and lit from within by tiny bulbs. They are sold in the millions by a company called "Department 56," which touched off a craze with its replication of small-town architecture found in the upper Midwest. The typical buyer—who, surprisingly, happens to be a middle-aged male invariably cites his desire to compensate for a world out of control when questioned about his affinity for this form of holiday decor. The hand can arrange and rearrange a toy town world at will; the miniaturization process at work in the villages permits a respite from the life of an on-the-road salesman or a harried office worker. Here order, peace, and ultimate personal control prevail.

As these examples suggest, alterations in scale and seasonal changes in familiar places are important to individuals and to the polity as a whole. Whether those changes mean putting a massive Christmas tree in Rockefeller Center or in one's own living room, or shrinking down reality to the manageable size of a dollhouse, these are

J. C. Nichols, Country Club Plaza, Kansas City. Contemporary view of shopping center designed in 1922.

crucial aesthetic principles that are relevant to the idea of architourism and escape.

One of the most familiar of all escapist environments is the movie theater. The architectural techniques used in today's post-postmodern theater complexes go back to the little Main Street movie house of a bygone era: the Rialto, the Venetian, the Rex, each with its appropriate make-believe decor, barely hinted at by the name on the marquee.

Today, a pseudo-Egyptoid tomb may front on the parking lot of a movie/video game center right next door to a Burger King. Once past the lotus-capital columns, you find yourself in an electrified temple at Luxor. Buying popcorn becomes a transformative experience. Ten minutes earlier you were arguing with your bratty teenager in the comfort of your new SUV; suddenly, you're in an old curse-of-the-Pharaoh movie, in real life, and that life is wonderful, if a little creepy.

Extending the cinematic experience is Jon Jerde's CityWalk, atop Universal City in Los Angeles. The site is on the border between Toluca Lake and Burbank, home of the old movie stars of the 1950s. One of the many things going on at City Walk is the transformation of the image of the city into a cinematic tourist attraction. Generations of pundits have bewailed the fact that Los Angeles is a mere collection of suburbs, a city without a city. So Jerde created one, with a host of extra added movieland attractions. Giant gorillas that hang off the facades of the business district. Hypertrophic palm trees. Cars that burst through walls as if architecture were just another kind of flimsy movie set or another kind of special effect. It's illusion, deliberate fakery, fun. The ultimate architecture of escape, or the "real" world cinematized.

Fun is not limited to Hollywood. A favorite tourist

mecca in the heartland is Country Club Plaza in Kansas City, built in the 1920s by J. C. Nichols, a developer who did not know he was making architourism history. His plaza is a shopping center designed for drivers. Hidden behind the neo-Spanish facades of the buildings are some of the first multilevel parking garages in America. But why modernity in a hacienda or an elegant casa? Through a fortuitous whim of the fates, Nichols and the local business community had linked up with an organization promoting Coronado Entrata, a multicity commemoration of the many places that Francisco Vásquez de Coronado had once visited, beginning at the Mexican border and moving through the now-United States. Coincidentally, Nichols found himself in Seville, in the heart of Spanish culture and architecture, and determined to recreate his experience on a swampy tract of land on the almost suburban fringe of Kansas City. From the day it opened, Country Club Plaza has been one of the most successful shopping complexes in the nation, partly because of the theming. It is one of the earliest examples of all-out, full-bore commercial theming (greatly enhanced by a dramatic Christmastime illumination). Peace in a Christmas village. Exoticism in a Kansas City shopping center

where a trip to Starbucks is a trip into history and some mythical Zorroland.

The Mall of America, in Bloomington, Minnesota, is only the latest example of the commercial as tourist attraction. It is also an escape. If Country Club Plaza turns a blazing Missouri summer into a sojourn in Old Spain, the Mall of America erases the rigors of the Minnesota winter (and the sizzle of summer). But in addition it illustrates the importance of surprise in architourism. From the outside, apart from a sign or two, the mall is nothing to look at: a big, bland box. Once inside, however, the humdrum box expands into a horizontal version of Trump Tower, a gaudy symphony in polished brass, blooming plants, atria, and every possible tone and texture of wall-to-wall carpeting. Somehow, magically, you have left Bloomington for New York, or California. Or no place on earth. And if that were not enough, there's a full-fledged Knott's Berry Farm amusement park in the center of mall, with carousels, flume rides, and a roller coaster. Space, time, and function all defy expectation.

Once inside, as customarily happens in well-designed casinos and supermarkets, the outside disappears. The magic act that made the parking lot

Camp Snoopy at the Mall of America. Photo: Jim Mone, AP Photo

disappear behind a berm or barrier of some kind owes a great deal to Walt Disney, who tried the trick first at Disneyland in 1955. Disney was also an undeclared enemy of the car and he devoted much of his later life to promoting various means of public transportation. Walking for pleasure—walking with others as a democratic experience—is another idea that Disney cherished. As a result of his efforts, pedestrianism is a major component of tourist architecture today. We don't walk to the supermarket much; we get in the car, unless we're New Yorkers, that is. Disney made recreational walking a desirable ingredient of tourism. In order to do so, he needed architectural forms and details sensitive to pedestrianism: things to look at, polished show windows, color-coordinated facades, awnings. Nothing is too pretty, too elaborate, or even too wild in the world of architourism, so long as there is something wonderful to see.

The Disney theme parks in recent years have also created places premised on the notion of displacement. In the 1980s, when plans were drawn up for a new park at Walt Disney World in Orlando, Florida, called the MGM Studios Attraction, the Imagineers (imagination + engineering = a vintage Waltism) decided to create an homage to Walt Disney's ideal Los Angeles. The founder used to love to prowl the city on foot in the late 1930s and 1940s, taking in the palm trees and the sunshine like a typical Midwesterner transplanted to paradise. Disney employees, in the company of local architectural critics and historians, began to photograph the old Art Deco commercial infrastructure, which was being destroyed at an alarming rate during the run-up to the new Florida environment. Their photographs, in turn, became the plans for the MGM Studios park, with the buildings spruced up and then approximated at a slightly reduced scale. What an outrageous and audacious scheme: to recreate glamorous Los Angeles, circa 1941, in the middle of Florida, circa 1991. Magic.

Los Angeles at the outset of America's participation in World War II may not look ideal to the historian. The fear of possible attacks on the West

Coast and the imprisonment of Japanese-Americans are two aspects of the period that seem difficult to celebrate. But the tourist inclined to revisit those historical episodes has ample opportunity to do so elsewhere. MGM is about assembling a set of memories selected for their ability to please, about giving the visitor the challenge of dating an experience through details of architecture and signage. It is less about reality than it is about fantasy, much like the Hollywood movies celebrated in the mini-Graumann's Chinese Theatre, which serves as the centerpiece of the park.

My intent here has been to suggest that escape is not always "escape from." It is also "escape to," or the notion of transformation as pleasure and possibility. If we are too formally or ideologically detached from the ways in which tourists use theme parks and malls and the like, we miss the point. One of the things I've always noticed at the Mall of America and the Disney venues is the smiling faces. These smiles are not on the faces of ignorant dopes consuming architecture (or baked goods) like so many rats in a maze. They are walking and looking with real pleasure at things—facades, simulations, wishes captured in brick and mortar (or fiberglass)— that they would otherwise not have a chance to see. Tourists are being displaced from their ordinary realities. And they are happy.

KELLER EASTERLING
NORTH KOREA LOVE BOAT

As a collection of fictions with no reckoning other than a price tag, tourism may also be a tool with political instrumentality—an instrument of diplomacy as well as a target and instrument of war. Fiction, the cheerful friend of politics and tourism, generates what the sociologist Pierre Bourdieu has called "symbolic capital"—a set of rituals and practices that provide not only social bonds but economic indicators, not because the comedy of its fake crests, seals, and epaulets actually means something, but precisely because they mean nothing, and there is a tacit agreement that they mean nothing. Tourism often provides a set of absurdist gestures that stand for something with shared meaning, a cultural gibberish reliant on the complete obfuscation of meaning.

This is tourism's sleight of hand, the means by which it floats irreconcilable fictions over a revenue stream. Filled with so much elaborate fiction, it provides the perfect opportunity for playacting, for loudly chanting beliefs while looking the other way as they are unenforced. It is another agreement to enter another global spectacle, another mercantile sovereignty in which both sides pretend to be what the other wants just long enough to make the deal.

Tourist ventures that have arrived late to the shores of twentieth-century combat or Cold War deadlock provide a broad cartoon of this political instrumentality. Tourism has found points of entry in countries like Vietnam and Cuba, sometimes landing on almost the very battle lines of separation. Perhaps one of the most extreme examples of this phenomenon has been Hyundai's tourist resort on Mount Kumgang in North Korea (DPRK) and the *I Love Cruise* that initiated it.

The *I Love Cruise,* now replaced by an overland route, was just the first step in an ongoing negotiation on tourism between North and South Korea that has created a "special tourist zone" near Mount Kumgang—Korea's spiritual equivalent of Mount Fuji, just north of the demilitarized zone and unseen by South Koreans since the mid-twentieth century. Kim Jong Il, "Respected and Beloved General" of North Korea's oxymoronic communist dynasty, and Chong Ju Yung, head of the South's Hyundai *chaebol,* initiated this tourist enterprise in 1998 under the auspices of the South's Sunshine Policy promoting reunification between the North and the South.[1]

Complete with karaoke and Siberian dancing girls, the cruise traveled at night via international waters, to rendezvous at dawn with North Korean warships. Each vessel was escorted to the top-secret military port of Changjon, near Mount Kumgang. Passengers then disembarked for a cycle of spa treatments and hiking tours of spectacular waterfalls, mountain peaks, and seascapes. In the tourist compound that still serves the resort today, the Pyongyang circus performed in a domed theater, and tourists could shop from a new line of North Korean products, including an ant liquor purported to cure impotence. From the tour buses, visitors could just see over the walls of the resort

compound to the declining agricultural villages that surrounded it. Among the fleet of cruise ships was the original *Island Princess*, which appeared in the television series *The Love Boat*.[2]

In this escape to a communist theme park, guards stationed at two-kilometer intervals along the resort's walls and hiking routes discourage picture taking, powerful lenses on cameras or binoculars, short skirts, and both American and Japanese flags. Also, carved into the mountainside are the poems of Kim Jong Il and the aphorisms of Juche, North Korea's cultlike philosophy of self-reliance, which combines the political dictates of Stalinism with Confucian traditions and the general outlines of missionary Christianity, and offers gently violent motivations that have coached the North Koreans through grinding poverty and famine.[3] It was anticipated that by 2005, a forty-five-hole golf course, casinos, theme parks, Hilton hotels, information technology campuses, and other amenities would stretch north from Mount Kumgang all along the eastern seaboard of the Korean peninsula to Mount Paektu, attracting an estimated 1.5 million tourists per year.

A telling proviso of the initial Kumgang deal was that Hyundai agreed to supply Kim Jong Il and his senior administration with 30,000 twenty-five-inch color television sets newly branded with a Kumgansan-Mount Kumgang label, thus disguising their identity as South Korean products. This comfort with laundered identities and forbidden desires was not prompted simply by Kim Jong Il's love of television. Rather, North Korea was to receive almost one hundred million dollars from Hyundai over six years, money that ostensibly was to be funneled into propping up the North's depleted economy (there has been some speculation that it went into Bureau 39, a Hong Kong bank account for a communist party organization). Another notable component of the deal was that Hyundai was to be granted oil-drilling rights in the North.

Kim Jong Il and Chong Ju Yung, both born in the mountain ranges on the east coast of North Korea, lent myths to the increasing number of fables and

A ship from the *I Love Cruise* fleet. Courtesy Hyundai-Asan

Accommodations for the _I Love Cruise_ included a floating hotel. Courtesy Hyundai-Asan

a benign paramilitary organization led by new recruits from the schools of hotel management and designed to conquer a market share of the landed hotel industry. Repeat customers support the industry, finding in it another escape from the interior of their own stories to a libidinized hyperdomesticity where everything is clean, someone else is cooking, and there is shopping. At Mount Kumgang, this conveniently locationless revenue format—one that flies many flags—was in the service of something else. Here, _The Love Boat_ meets a wholesome militarized version of reality television.

With the help of laundered identities, fiction, and disguise, the "I Love Cruise" and the evolving Kumgang resort have amounted to a global handshake that synchronizes the disparate logics of shamanism, communism, Confucianism, neo-Christian mythology, Juche, and capitalism. The choreographed activities of tourism merge with the choreography of a communist state. North Korea now uses not only nuclear weapons as pawns of extortion and brinkmanship but also a special pirate space with its own temporary amnesties from socialist principles.

Bargaining with extrapolitical territories, such as free-trade zones, casinos, airports, duty-free shops, and cruise ships, is part of the repertoire of not only transnational corporations but also rogue nations. A country in need of food, roads, telephones, electricity, and up-to-date factories has, in this deal, escaped into the slushiest vein of revenue and the most extravagant stratum of global spectacles with its special tourist zone, or STZ. While it may dramatize the production of the industrial or agricultural worker, North Korea has transferred its faith to the tourist, the gambler, and the information specialist. It has discovered the resort and the information technology campus as new factories of production. Ironically, North Korea maintains self-respect partly by sampling and denigrating an alien culture even while it accepts profits from it—not unlike the husband who can more easily have an affair with an interloper, a _femme fatale_, than with his neighbor's wife.

No longer a tentative experiment, the Kumgang

fictions that surround the story of the resort. As legend goes, Kim Jong Il was born in the presence of a star and three elderly men on Mount Paektu. The Horatio Alger-like Chong Ju Yung, born a peasant near Kumgang, rose to become an American-style postwar industrialist and a twenty-first-century globalization logician. Both characters made Mount Kumgang the symbol of their respective cults of mid-twentieth-century modernity.

Cruising itself is a cult of sorts that adds further hyperbole to the stories emanating from both democracy and communism. The television series _The Love Boat,_ on which the "I Love Cruise" was based, was the single most important explanation for the success of cruising as a mass-market product in the 1970s. This television cruise space functions like

development has continued to expand. Family reunions, suspended after September 11, 2001, have resumed, and there is now an online visa-processing site.[4] In September 2002, work began on a link between the Seoul-Sinuiju and Onjong-ri (at the foot of Mount Kumgang) rail lines and Chojin; the overland route opened in February 2003. In the fall of 2002, a South Korean chain was permitted to open its first two convenience stores on Mount Kumgang, and two restaurants opened that winter.[5] In addition to renovating the hotel, Hyundai has been given permission to erect temporary tourist bungalows around the newly built spa.[6] Hyundai is also to begin work on two golf courses, a ski lift, and a Bungee jump.[7]

The DPRK claims to favor the entry of technological innovation, while filtering out other bad habits of the market, yet it continues to embark on far stranger adventures with capitalism. There is still no television or Internet connection with the outside world for most of the country, but the opening of three hundred large markets, forty of which are in Pyongyang, has been largely publicized.[8] The Unification Church, which had originally made a bid for the Kumgang project, has entered into an agreement with Fiat to build an automobile factory in the North, the Peace Motor Company, that will produce a jeep as the first affordable, "middle-class" car. Hyundai is also slated to build sixteen automobile factories in the North as well as a technology park just north of the demilitarized zone.[9] The park echoes technology complexes in North America and around the world, with a proposed name of "Mount Kumgang Valley."[10]

Neither reasonable procedures and principled stances using classic political tools, nor even neoliberal programs characterize the success of Hyundai's resort venture and cruise ship, which with its promiscuity and luxury, was able to slither through the jurisdictional shallows and penetrate the most reclusive nation on earth. The resort is a Mata Hari that has become a space for political summits, meetings of the Red Cross, and family

Mt. Kumgang promotional material. Courtesy Hyundai-Asan

reunions. Two kinds of escape are in play for both cruises and rogue nations: the escape to an interior free of contradictory information and the escape to a space of disguise and fiction swimming between contradictory logics.

In other former Cold War hot spots, tourism also purports to be the quick, almost universal, cultural

entente and revenue stream. For instance, tourist ventures have sprung up in what used to be North and South Vietnam. In the waters surrounding Cuba, waters that, for centuries, were infested with pirates and recently have been the site of Cold War skirmishes, the seaside resort of Varadero, just across the island from the Bay of Pigs, is an enclave not unlike Kumgang. Frequented by Canadians and Europeans, it is only a two-hour drive from Havana and features a number of hotels, restaurants, and nightclubs that most Cubans cannot afford. Fidel Castro has touted Cuba as a nation whose tourism offers "peace, health, and security,"[11] with an emphasis on security. The Cold War nation is a safe place, a nostalgic combat site, with 1957 Chevrolets and quaint touches of both modernism and communism, such as the Hotel Habana Libre, formerly the Havana Hilton.

Thus tourism functions as a Vatican-like state within a state, offering political asylum, internal escape, and immunity to all converts who would recognize and endorse its images. The tourist industry indexes the world by flight times from major cities, beachside water temperature, days of sunlight, quality of sand, and length of stay. Its spatial products are designed to be free to spread into growing territory unencumbered by political inconveniences like taxes and local laws, and the spin that accompanies them bathes them in peaceful neutrality.

And yet it is the attempt to escape political consequence that also often puts tourism in the crosshairs of political conflict, so that it actually becomes not a tool for negotiating peace but a target of war. The 2002 terrorist bombings in Bali made clear that tourist installations are not merely politically neutral, "Third-Way" revenue streams but also tantalizing signals of an arrogant belief in political immunity and superiority, especially when the political stakes are culturally foreign. The recent bombings in the Sinai were targeted at Israelis who were attempting a temporary escape from the violence at home.[12] In their lack of overt political text, their association with nature and peaceful cultural exchange, tourism is the perfect target, the perfect

unexpected shock in the terrorist script.

In the escapism and amnesties of tourism's pirate space lie powerful political mechanisms that, when deliberately manipulated, transport the tale not to the style pages but to the fictions of the international pages. Architecture and urbanism are critical pawns in a game within which tourism's supposed political neutrality is actually at the heart of its political instrumentality.

NOTES

1. The Sunshine Policy was a South Korean plan to promote economic cooperation between North and South Korea. Marcus Noland, *Avoiding the Apocalypse: The Future of the Two Koreas* (Washington, D.C.: Institute for International Economics, 2000), 85; and "Ships of Capitalism Sail into the Myths," *International Herald Tribune*, March 11, 2000, 7.

2. See various newspaper accounts of the Kumgang resort and the" I Love Cruise," especially: "Kumgang Tour Shows North Korea's Beauty, Isolation," *New York Times*, April 23, 2000, 5H; "High Wire Feats Rule North Korea," *New York Times*, March 13, 2000, 1E; "North Korea Opens Its Door, Just a Crack," *New York Times*, March 7, 2000, 1C; "See North—But No Photos Please." *Toronto Star*, June 9, 2000; and " Vacationers in North Korea Kept in Their Place," *New York Times*, January 20, 2002, A10.

3. Kongdan Oh and Ralph C. Hassig, *North Korea through the Looking Glass* (Washington, D.C.: Brookings Institution Press, 2000), 33.

4. "South Korea to process online visa applications to North," *BBC Worldwide Monitoring*, November 7, 2002.

5. "Trial Runs of a Free Market in North Korea," *New York Times*, March 11, 2003, C1.

6. "Koreas: North to Designate Mt. Kumgang Special Tourism Zone," *BBC Worldwide Monitoring*, October 30, 2002; "Koreas: South Company Opens Shop at North's Mt Kumgang Tourist Spot," *BBC Worldwide Monitoring*, November 6, 2002.

7. "Trial Runs of a Free Market in North Korea," *New York Times*, March 11, 2003, C1.

8. "Inter-Korea economic meeting reaches agreement," *Xinhua General News Service*, November 19, 2003; *The News Hour with Jim Lehrer*, June 29, 2004.

9. "Unification Church to Build Autos in N. Korea," *The Daily Record*, Baltimore, January 18, 2000; *The News Hour with Jim Lehrer*, June 29, 2004.

10. "Trial Runs of a Free Market in North Korea," *New York Times*, March 11, 2003, C1; " North Korean Leader Said Considering Mt. Kumgang Technology Complex," *BBC Monitoring International Reports*, April 20, 2004; "Hyundai to Develop Mt. Geumgang Area into Tourist Complex, IT Zone," *Korea Times*, November 25, 2002.

11. "Cuba—Tourism Cuba Registers Record High Number of Tourists During High Season," *Global New Wire*, EFE News Services, May 4, 2003.

12. "Israelis Trudge Home, in Shock After Bombings," *New York Times*, October 9, 2004.

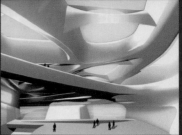

DETOUR
RIO DE JANEIRO, BRAZIL; TAICHUNG, TAIWAN...

In the wake of its success in Bilbao, the Guggenheim Foundation has floated plans to build satellite museums in a growing number of cities around the globe from Europe and the United States to Latin America and Asia. Guggenheim director Thomas Krens's appreciation for showy starchitecture is matched by his expansionist ambitions to make his institution a ubiquitous brand. Among the places most recently added to the Guggenheim list, besides Hong Kong and Guadalajara (see related projects on pages 103 and 142), are Rio de Janeiro, Taichung, Guangzhou, Macau, Shanghai, and Singapore. Increasingly, however, the "Bilbao effect" has come to grief on the shoals of "Guggenheim economics," as many of these cities have realized that the effect may not be so easy to achieve or may come at too high a cost.

With local variations, the Guggenheim business model depends on the satellite city funding the new museum and its building, plus paying the parent institution a fee for the use of its name. In return, the nascent museum gains access to loans of artwork from the Guggenheim's collection as well as to its traveling exhibitions, and receives management consultation. While the Guggenheim's prestige might further weight the deal favorably in places eager for cultural cachet, opponents have seen the strategy as a debt trap. Especially in already economically strapped locations, they have questioned whether the tremendous cash outlay required might not be better spent on improving urban services and infrastructure or alternatively on local arts initiatives and organizations. Not surprisingly, the specter of "cultural imperialism" has hung heavily over many of the debates.

In one of the more highly touted recent schemes, for Rio de Janeiro, Brazil, French architect Jean Nouvel proposed to partly submerge a cylindrical building in the waters of Guanabara Bay. Intended to revitalize a derelict dock area and to attract tourists on cruise ships, the project was likened by detractors to a huge, rusting oil drum. A legal battle ended with the court declaring it unlawful for the mayor to sign a contract with the Guggenheim since it entailed financial obligations beyond his term of office. Similarly, in Taichung, Taiwan, a design by architect Zaha Hadid for a structure with movable wings and floors, championed by another mayor, was dropped after the budget came in at twice the $120 million cost of Bilbao.

The Guggenheim has also been fighting battles at home. In January 2005 the museum's chairman of the board, Peter Lewis, resigned over the institution's overextended finances and Krens's franchise strategy for growth. Two years earlier it was forced to close an outpost in Las Vegas, designed by Rem Koolhaas, which opened shortly after September 11, 2001, and fell victim to a national downturn in tourism. A major project by Frank Gehry himself for a second Guggenheim in New York City, close to the site of the World Trade Center, was also left in limbo after the terrorist attacks. The tenacious Krens currently has his eye on another New York site, the Hudson Yards on Manhattan's West Side, where the city is trying to push through plans for a new football stadium.

Top, project by Zaha Hadid Architects, Taichung, Taiwan, 2003.
Bottom, project by Ateliers Jean Nouvel, Rio de Janeiro, Brazil, 2003.

SILVIA KOLBOWSKI
SOMETHING FOR NOTHING

1996
Stills from DVD, 7 minutes

The video loop combines a view of the Las Vegas casino strip shot from a car
with running text taken from descriptions of high-design products that
appeared in a contemporaneous issue of *Domus* magazine. Jean-François
Lyotard has noted that the old legitimization of capitalism—"everyone will get
rich"—is no longer believable. But businesses boom at particular moments,
for particular reasons. The casino is a throwback to a "get-rich" narrative at
the level of play. Casinos are tourism and entertainment containers par
excellence because they benefit from the sense of suspended time that the
nonplace provides. The excitement of open sight lines is contained by a
scintillating skin that keeps out the banality of the car traffic of the Strip. The
punishing odds against winning add to the ultimate capitalist fantasy—getting
something for nothing.

The video is part of a larger project conceived for the "Containers" section
of the exhibition *Present and Futures: Architecture in Cities,* organized by
Ignasi de Solà-Morales and Xavier Costa at the Centre de Cultura
Contemporánea, Barcelona, in 1996.

ed aluminum tubing - glossy

ANETTE BALDAUF AND DORIT MARGREITER
REMAKE LAS VEGAS

2001–2
DVD, 18 minutes

In 2001 Las Vegas began a mission to transform itself into a real city. On the Strip
the Venetian hotel complex opened a Guggenheim Museum franchise designed by
Rem Koolhaas and Frank Gehry, while downtown Mayor Oscar Goodman proposed
a new art museum to spur a more sophisticated metropolitan ambiance. With this
introduction of the currency of art, the googie Strip and the previously neglected
downtown area began to compete over "authentic" urbanity.

How seamlessly can art be integrated into the entertainment industry? Will
museums fill the gap between high and low culture, between entertainment and
everyday life?

Kurt Ouchida
The Venetian

Marjorie Polly, Earl White
Downtown Cultural Development Committee

Guggenheim Las Vegas   (Big Box)

GUGGENHEIM
LAS VEGAS

SPECTACULAR

SPECTACULAR SPECTACULAR!

Nowadays, the exclamation "Spectacular!" (or "Spectacular Spectacular!" as hyped in Baz Luhrmann's recent film *Moulin Rouge*) tends to draw the lines of the taste-culture battle, rather than bring to mind the image of Carmen Miranda, the "Lady in the Tutti Frutti Hat," or express our ecstasy at the bedazzling showstoppers of Cecil B. DeMille and Busby Berkeley and their architectural equivalents—those wish-images of a long-lost age of innocence. The adjective, of course, summons into play the "spectacle," a key concept for analyzing the condition of art and architecture in the era of the mass media, a condition famously—and negatively—diagnosed by Guy Debord, first in *The Society of the Spectacle* (1967) and again, some twenty years later, in *Comments on the Society of the Spectacle* (1988). In *Comments*, Debord registers what he regarded as the terminal stage of the society of the spectacle, indicating how the earlier twentieth-century forms of spectacular power—the "diffuse spectacle" of American capitalism and the "concentrated spectacle" of totalitarianism—have become conflated in the "integrated spectacle" that imposes itself globally. In his Marxist critique of advanced capitalism, the spectacle is not simply a reference to the mass media but a totalizing figure that describes the entire ensemble of social, political, and cultural relations under capitalism and, as a corollary, the subject's complete inscription within and domination by spectacular relations.

Debord's anatomy of the mechanisms of the spectacle and their aesthetic and ideological effects is a denunciation of the alienation caused by a society based on commodity production and the false subjectivity of commodity fetishism. According to Debord, the society of the spectacle reduces visuality to a form of domination, and as a result, spectatorship is immediately equated with passivity and the manufactured and thus artificial agency of consumption. Debord locates in the spectacle's distraction an absolute form of alienated spectatorship that separates spectators from one another and from lived experience, which, in its spectacular representations, becomes the ultimate commodity in the circulation of capital. Walter Benjamin, on the other hand, in his essay "The Work of Art in the Age of Mechanical Reproduction" (1935), posits the notion of distracted spectatorship, which moves us partly away from the scopic and toward the haptic/tactile

and habitual/empirical consciousness. It is important to remember that Benjamin, even though his work precedes that of Debord, valorizes distracted spectatorship, regarding cinema and its regime of shocks, for example, as a way of generating a mass audience that is critical. For Benjamin, spectatorship is a two-way street. On the other hand, Debord writes, in *Comments on the Society of the Spectacle,* "spectacular discourse leaves no room for any reply." This positions the citizen-spectator as absolutely passive, taking away from him or her the minimal right of inspection, to say nothing of the possibility of "seeing through" spectacular discourse. Are we too mesmerized and dominated to rethink the mechanisms of spectacle culture in terms of the capacity of spectacle to have a critical and even liberating effect? Crucial to such a tack is the elaboration of a more articulated account of spectatorship, both individual and collective, than Debord offers, one that not only accounts for the eudaemonic of spectatorship—pleasure/bliss, voyeurism/fetishism—but also for the tasks of spectatorship that involve an active response to enunciative positioning, and that may also take the form of interactive and (counter-) participatory responses expressive of resistance and opposition.

Despite these qualifications, Debord's epochal critique inevitably imposes itself as a point of reference for a discussion dedicated to architecture-as-spectacle and to architecture as a tourist attraction, that is, an architecture intended from its very inception not only to enter the global Baedeker as an asterisked site/sight but also to re-map and to colonize the Baedeker itself in terms of architourism: *See Bilbao and die! See the New Forty-second Street and live!* But perhaps the real question to ask is whether contemporary architecture has the right to be spectacular: What is wrong with architecture's being spectacular— ecstatic, excessive, exorbitant, aestheticized, imagistic, seductive—in an eye-intensive culture that has transposed the exhibitionistic function of the architectural work into a secular version of the auratic, a cultic object for the new rite of global tourism? Or, to put this question the other way around: what is right with architecture's being spectacular? Can spectacularized architecture have a critical function? Can it use spectacle against spectacular culture and the forms of reception it imposes? These questions involve going beyond Debord and his avatars (Baudrillard, Neil Leach, and so on), although we now no longer know where we are in the evolution of the society of the spectacle or whether its interregnum is already in place. These questions may also be brought to bear upon the events of September 11, 2001, perhaps the most decisive event in the history of spectacle culture, one that has altered, once and for all, the way in which we may speak of "spectacular architecture" and the pleasure/bliss it confers. Indeed, the memorial to the World Trade Center towers threatens to become one more Station of the Cross in "Junkspace" (to borrow from Rem Koolhaas), commemorating architectural terrorism, the ultimate spectacle in our society of the spectacle, and memorializing the terrorists' hijacking of the master narrative of global spectacle culture according to a choreography that outdoes Hollywood's most apocalyptic disaster movie. Instead of performing its traditional mourning-work, architecture, in erecting the memorial, will perhaps perform mourning-work for itself.

ARCHITOURISM AND EMPIRE, OR IN THE BUFFALO SOUP

In *The Society of the Spectacle,* Debord also wrote critically of tourism as one more instance of spectacular separation and alienation produced by the banalization and homogenization of the built environment that dissipates the difference between space and place:

> Human circulation considered as something to be consumed—tourism—is a by-product of the circulation of commodities; basically, tourism is the chance to go and see what has been made trite. The economic management of travel to places suffices in itself to ensure those places' interchangeability. The same modernization that has deprived travel of its temporal aspect has likewise deprived it of the reality of space.[1]

Here Debord certainly anticipates our present moment of globalization in which cultural differences have become, in effect, liquidated, supplanted by those "little differences"—the Royale with cheese, Le Big Mac—memorialized by Quentin Tarantino in *Pulp Fiction.* These have come to characterize the hamburger-centric worldview of the new breed of innocents abroad, exponents of a lazy tourism no longer in search of difference and one that could just as easily be ventured through cyber-means. Tourism has become our dominant way of being in the world, whether at home or abroad. Tourism is the appropriate *habitus* for our excursions through Rem Koolhaas's Junkspace, the fabulous architectural detritus that now litters our urban and suburban surround. Junkspace is the built environment through which the world is spectacularized according to the "anaesthetics" (Leach) of postmodernist urbanism and architecture, a cross between Disneyland delirium and the Bilbao effect. When operating within it, we become (accidental) architourists at every moment of our existence, roaming though a global theme park *qua* shopping mall that extends from Alaska to Patagonia.

What is the role that architecture is to assume with respect to both globalization, of which it is a primary instrument, and the hyper-aesthetics of the current installment of global culture—call it the culture of Empire or of MTV and the reality show gone cosmic or, as I prefer (following the filmmaker Robert Kramer), "Buffalo soup," that is, the spectacle culture of postmodernism, intensified and pumped up? It is possible to map out globalization in terms of the architectural extravaganzas that now punctuate its transnational Empire City, perhaps asterisking those works that maintain the independence and quality of place and community and that resist spectacular consumption and the consumption of architecture itself. As a corrective gesture, it would also be possible to counter-map globalization in terms of the mega-slum it has created and the catastrophe of urban poverty that is its underside, as Mike Davis has recently done.[2] The global 'hood is the by-product of globalization, and it is at once refractory and porous to it—infiltrated by the signifiers and commodities of global culture. But however corrective and sobering such a counter-mapping may be, it is ultimately futile. Even the slum has become spectacularized within the urban imaginary of Empire. Here I am thinking particularly of contemporary film, that is, the newly globalized cinema that has displaced national cinemas and has amalgamated and appropriated the languages of cultural and cinematic

otherness through which those national cinemas, particularly their peripheral production, formerly spoke. These appropriations, whether of the First or Third World, have yielded over the last decade or so a body of slum films that, with good intentions, treat the actual conditions of our "planet of slums." They employ, however, the transnational style through which much of contemporary cinema speaks. That amped-up, hotted-up, and accelerated style has been described in terms of its "intensive continuity," to use David Bordwell's term, although it could just as well be called intensive discontinuity, given its extensive use of violent or electronic cutting. Consider, for example, *The City of God* (2002), a slum film in the form of a gangster movie made by the Brazilian filmmaker Fernando Meirelles. The question that the film implicitly puts to its spectator at every moment of viewing is the following: Are we dealing with a spectacular slum, a slum spectacularized by the exorbitant cinematic language of a virtuoso postmodernist *auteur* whose style, honed by a long apprenticeship in television and television commercials, is in keeping with the Buffalo soup aesthetics of global hyper-cinema? Or are we in an authentic social-problem film that deploys a *vérité* style capable of anatomizing in a critical way the brutalizing urban conditions at work in the gangland of the city of god, a shantytown located on the periphery of Rio? At certain points throughout the film, I found my delirium interrupted by disorienting and contradictory border-crossings and code-switches. Was I watching a Brazilian film or a transnational, transcontinental American movie, stylistically closer to Boyz N the Hood than to the favela films of Fernando Birri and Perreira dos Santos and the other original proponents of Third Cinema? In what filmic urban imaginary was I—that of the planet of slums or that of Planet Hollywood? For sure, I was in the global 'hood, the same carceral, ultra-violent, and soul-murdering third space that has been charted cinematically by a number of other contemporary filmmakers, for example, Mira Nair in *Salaam Bombay!* and Antonio Capuano in *Vito e gli Altri* (along with the other Neapolitan filmmakers of the new *lazaronitum*), and, most important, by a tribe of American "mean street" filmmakers, both African-American and Caucasian. Indeed, the intertextuality between *City of God* and Martin Scorsese's *Good Fellas* has become a commonplace in the film's critical reception, as have comparisons with *Gangs of New York* and *Pulp Fiction.* So, for sure, I was in the Empire of Cinema. Perhaps an allegory of architourism can be found in such cinematic "slumming" in an Empire in which the global 'hood and the global village are the same destination.

By way of concluding, I offer a series of architectural questions to be accompanied by the refrain of the *Buffalo Soup Blues*:

Does architecture need to treat the issue of spectacle and its current institutional inscription within spectacle culture directly? Do architects, in their buildings, need to take up consciously a position either for or against the spectacularization of architecture? And to question this question: is responding to spectacularization in such a polemical—either/or—way just one more ideological exercise in applying frames of acceptance or rejection, when, in fact, a much more complex attitude is required? Is a critique of

architecture-as-spectacle possible? Is it possible to use architecture to level a critique against spectacle culture and the *habitus* it has imposed upon architecture and the agency of the architect?

Has the so-called Bilbao effect had an impact—positive or negative—on architectural practice(s) and architecture's self-conception? In some respects, it seems to resemble the blockbuster syndrome that Hollywood has imposed on its filmmakers since the 1970s, something that has had dire results, producing, on one hand, the cinema of directorial megalomania and, on the other, the cinema of sameness, which has led to the death of the art film, the cinema that does rigorous work on language. Beneath the question of the Bilbao effect lies the issue of what may be called the "Frank Gehry effect"—the abiding problem of the architect's signature and the architectural politics of the proper name. Has the Gehry effect initiated a new era of architectural auteurism, and if so, how is this to be regarded? Is all the recent talk about "archityranny" on the mark?

Can the notion of architourism be applied to the specifics of architectural design and its reception? The architect, in designing a building intended to serve as a tourist destination, endows the building with a number of touristic functions that may go beyond the general aestheticization and spectacularization of the site. Increasingly seen is the phenomenon of the building as an architectural *tour de force* that requires its visitor to experience it through the mediation of an audio-tour. Does the architect simply regard the tourist as a potential sightseer who will experience the building in a serendipitous and, at times, distracted way, or does the architect project into the program the figure of the tourist as a model spectator (user/consumer/reader) who needs to be positioned and guided so that the building can function to maximum effect? There is an extensive literature—from Dean MacCannell to John Urry—dedicated to profiling the competence (the ad hoc semiotics, for one) and the architectural desire of the mass tourist. But what kind of intentionality—or lack thereof—can be ascribed to the mass tourist, who usually experiences architecture as part of a collectivity? Is the contemporary architourist more of a "site-seer" than a sightseer—no longer Benjamin's distracted spectator but someone prepared to be "blown away" by the architectural event and primed to have the peak experience of brand-name architecture? How does an architecture programmed for the tourist differ from one addressed to the "ordinary" user/consumer (no easy question given the fact that all of us— Nowherians—have become tourists, even in our home cities)? If we can speak of archityranny, we can also speak of the dictatorship of a tourist industry and culture that demands comfort-zoned and predictably spectacular architecture: the architecture of pleasure as opposed to the architecture of bliss, to summon into play Roland Barthes's always useful distinction.

But such questions, if they are to have any efficacy, need to be applied to the specifics of processing the architectural text. To reiterate: does the "architecture of attractions" require the architect to build into the architectural object and its urban context a specific program of response geared to a tourist mode of perception and reception—specifically, the tourist

gaze? Does the architect need to embed within a program a specific itinerary of spectatorship that privileges the visual dimension of the building? Does that itinerary conflict or coincide with the haptic and tactile reception of the building? What sort of tasks can be imposed upon the tourist who comes to architecture not only as a sightseer but equipped with a camera and, even when without a camera, with the eye of a camera disposed toward quick takes? How can the tourist be made to assume a contemplative stance toward architecture or engage in a slow or interrogative reading of the site? Is it possible to convert the universal tourist from sightseeing to site-seeing? Or are these old-fashioned questions totally irrelevant to an architecture conceived and executed as entertainment?

PELLEGRINO D'ACIERNO

NOTES
1. Guy Debord, *The Society of the Spectacle*, translated by Donald Nicholson-Smith (New York: Zone Books, 1995), 120.

2. See Mike Davis, "Planet of Slums," *New Left Review* 26 (March–April 2004), 5–34.

JVC CENTER
TEN ARQUITECTOS
GUADALAJARA, MEXICO, 1998–

key:
1 TEN Arquitectos
2 Carme Piños
3 Morphosis
4 Coop Himmelb(l)au
5 Philip Johnson
6 Toyo Ito
7 Jean Nouvel

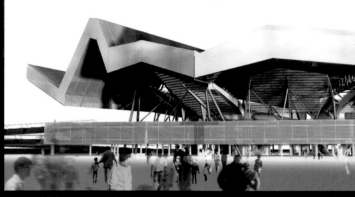

Clockwise from top left: Carme Piños, fairgrounds; Morphosis, palenque; Jean Nouvel, office complex; Philip Johnson, children's museum; Toyo Ito, museum of contemporary art.

TEN Arquitectos was also commissioned to design JVC's approximately 1.5-million-square-foot Convention and Exhibition Center. The specification of a multifunctional, free-span assembly space to accommodate 20,0000 spectators on its upper level led to the concept of a dome.

The plan, in turn, is defined by a series of concentric ellipses, which produce a multilevel building inside the dome and accommodate the complex functional demands while serving as structural support for the dome's very fine and light space-frame structure.

Three 200,000-square-foot exhibition spaces are stacked on top of each other, occupying the center of the ellipses. The exhibition spaces are surrounded by various spatial layers containing mechanical and support areas, conference and meeting rooms, two auditoriums, a cafeteria, banquet hall, ballrooms, offices, and service areas. The outermost ellipse defines the visitors' multilevel circulation paths, which are keyed by color coding based on the solar spectrum. This adds to the rich interstitial experience of the building, the dome's structure, and the surrounding landscape.

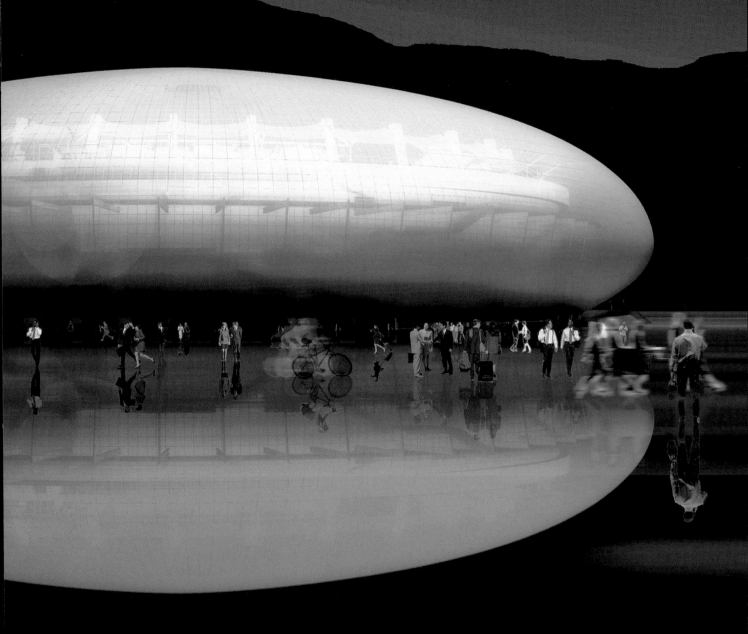

The theme for the Paris International Exposition 2004 (Expo 2004) was the image in all its manifestations. The unifying spatial concept of the master-plan design was thus the juxtaposition of different kinds of images—moving versus surface, part versus whole, and images that shock versus smoothly continuous filmic images. These images in turn were broken down into composite elements—namely, points, lines, grids, frames, and pixels. These image elements had architectural analogues in the components of the master plan, which included a central court, gates, bridges, national pavilions, kiosks, and an auditorium, all located on a 125-acre site in Seine St. Denis, a community just north of Paris.

The design for Expo 2004 created a setting that transcended the static, pictorial characteristics of the image by addressing the realm of the imaginary. An effort was made to invent a coherent and precise device to transport the public toward a new dimension—the meeting point between real and virtual worlds. The goal was not to immerse the spectator in a world of images, but instead to enable him or her to become an active mediator in the displacement between the real and virtual.

BLUR BUILDING
DILLER + SCOFIDIO
YVERDON-LES-BAINS, SWITZERLAND, 2002

The Blur Building was an exhibition pavilion built for Swiss Expo 2002 on Lake Neuchâtel in the town of Yverdon-les-Bains. It was an architecture of atmosphere. The lightweight tensegrity structure measured 300 feet wide by 200 feet deep by 75 feet high for a total of 80,000 square feet. The primary building material, water, was indigenous to the site. Water was pumped from the lake, filtered, and shot as a fine mist through a dense array of 31,500 high-pressure mist nozzles. The resulting fog mass produced a dynamic interplay of natural and man-made forces. A smart weather system read the shifting climatic conditions of temperature, humidity, wind speed, and wind direction, and processed the data in a central computer that regulated water pressure to the nozzles.

Four hundred visitors could occupy the building at any time. Upon entering the fog mass, visual and acoustic references were erased, leaving only an optical "white-out" and the "white-noise" of pulsing nozzles. Blur was an anti-spectacle. Contrary to immersive environments that strive for high-definition visual fidelity with ever-greater technical virtuosity, Blur was decidedly low-definition: there was nothing to see but our dependence on vision itself.

Unlike a conventional building, Blur was a habitable medium—one that was spaceless, formless, featureless, depthless, scaleless, massless, surfaceless, and dimensionless. On the platform, movement was unregulated and the public was free to wander in an immersive acoustic environment, designed by Christian Marclay. From the platform, the public ascended a stair to the Angel Deck at the summit. Emerging through the fog was like piercing a cloud layer while in flight to the blue sky. Submerged one half-level below the deck was the Water Bar, which offered a broad selection of bottled waters from around the world.

JOAN OCKMAN
BESTRIDE THE WORLD LIKE A COLOSSUS: THE ARCHITECT AS TOURIST

In 1995 Rem Koolhaas embarked on a "pure research project" in collaboration with his architecture students at Harvard. Its purpose was to investigate the issues and conditions surrounding the "urban mutations" taking place throughout the world in recent years.[1] Two volumes in a projected series of megabooks have appeared so far: *Harvard Design School Guide to Shopping* and *Great Leap Forward* (both 2001). These deal with, respectively, the past, present, and future of shopping in relation to architecture, offering an apocalyptic scenario based on the notion that everything is morphing into the space of commerce; and the Pearl River Delta, a corner of southeast China reaching from Hong Kong to Macau that is caught up in a similarly all-engulfing "maelstrom of modernization" and slated to have 34 million inhabitants by 2020.[2]

The third volume will be about Lagos, Nigeria, and occasioned a series of field trips to that city. In lectures about the project and a full-length documentary film made in 2003, Koolhaas has acknowledged that the motivation for a white middle-aged architect like himself to focus on an African city like Lagos at this moment may be less than self-evident, particularly as it is not a matter of his having a commission to design anything there. Plagued by endemic corruption, crime, and dysfunctional infrastructure during the 1990s, the city has had a reputation for being the most dangerous in the world as well as one of the most chaotic. But beyond a perverse curiosity regarding an alien and remote place, Koolhaas states, "we had an intuition"—he characteristically uses the royal or editorial pronoun—"that Lagos was becoming an important city [and] we wanted to be the first to understand how it works."[3]

Rem Koolhaas in Lagos. Stills from the documentary film *Lagos/Koolhaas,* 2002

Indeed, not just Lagos's recent explosive growth but its propensity for entrepreneurial improvisation and, despite the anarchic appearances, "self-organization" are what have particularly attracted the Dutch architect, who professes to be seeking in his own design practice "to develop more informal ways to plan cities."[4] Koolhaas has thus insisted that his mission is learning from Lagos rather than looking at it from a touristic perspective. "One thing that connects all our activities is [an interest in] modernization," he has explained. "That is what I've dedicated my life to."[5] Yet it is also evident that what has led him to its wild urbanism—armed with digital camera, film crew, Ivy League entourage, and the Nigerian president's helicopter—just as to China's construction boom and Prada's high-fashion runways, is an aesthetic and intellectual fascination with contemporary spectacles of global culture, whether of under- or overdevelopment.

We shall return to Koolhaas's project at the end of this essay. What is at stake more generally here is a subject that has received fragmentary attention to date: the architect as a tourist or, in a larger sense, as an observer of the world. The sociologist John Urry has defined the "tourist gaze" in his book of that title as the way societies and social groups view places different from those typically encountered in daily life. Following Foucault's work on the medical gaze in *The Birth of the Clinic,* Urry argues that the tourist gaze is constructed and systematized by institutions and norms that regulate the relationship between everyday and "other" experience.[6]

The architect's gaze too is a product of these discursive formations as well as practices, conventions, and codes specific to architecture as a discipline and profession. These affect the way architects see the world, think about it, and translate their experience into built form. Above all, the privileging of sight over the other senses in Western metaphysics since Plato and the increasing technical rationalization of this faculty since the beginning of the modern epoch have influenced habits of architectural perception and cognition. As such, forms of architectural spectatorship associated with clear subject-object boundaries, critical detachment or "perspective," and rationalized standards of measurement and representation have tended to be valued over those that are immersive, multisensorial, and intuitive.

The architect is also an expert. Unlike the "everyday" or lay observer, who, relatively speaking, tends to experience the built environment in a distracted or absent-minded way, as Walter Benjamin suggests,[7] architects by training and trade look with attention and knowledge, even on vacation. Not surprisingly, they prefer to think of themselves more as travelers than tourists, a semantic distinction that carries a nuance of elitist disdain for the viewing habits and tastes of the less sophisticated. In their capacity as experts and intellectuals, they are engaged in reflecting and speculating upon, or theorizing, their surroundings. The word *theory* is etymologically rooted in seeing, as various commentators have pointed out. Related to the word *theater,* it comes from the Greek *teoria,* a looking at, viewing, attentive beholding. The *Oxford English Dictionary* gives the first definition of theory as "a sight, a spectacle," a meaning now rare or obsolete although extant in the Bible.

But most distinctively, architects are also aesthetic producers. They are not just engaged in mastering what they see by means of theorizing it (like social scientists, for example), but ultimately in remastering it as new architecture and planning. They thus differ from their fellow travelers by being active rather than passive spectators, observers for whom the consumption of places has a direct or indirect link to future production. As such, the architectural imagination has historically played a significant role within the "empire of the gaze."[8] From the Grand Tour to the present, whether motivated by a scientific search for knowledge, colonizing ambitions, romantic desires, or other impulses, architect-tourists have both reflected the worldview of their time and literally constructed it.

Robert Adam, a Scottish architect who embarked on a Grand Tour to France, Italy, and the Dalmatian coast in 1754 at the age of twenty-six, was an exemplary figure in this tradition. Combining the attributes of student, well-to-do traveler, explorer, collector, and scientific observer, he embodied the archaeological and antiquarian interests of his day. Upon arriving in Spalatro (present-day Split), he undertook to survey and catalogue the remains of Diocletian's Palace with such zeal that the Venetian governor there accused him of being involved in espionage. After returning to Britain, his studies and reconstructions of ancient monuments, including a magisterial folio on Diocletian's Palace published a decade later, vastly expanded the British repertory of classical knowledge. Even more significant historically, though, was the new spirit of freedom and fantasy that he admitted into his own designs, which were based on classical models. In part inspired by Piranesi, whose acquaintance he had made in Rome, in part by the intimate familiarity with the originals he had acquired on his tour, he and his brother James revolutionized British taste for a generation.

As this example suggests, the theory of the gaze is not fully adequate to account for epochal shifts in the architect's ingrained habits of perception and cognition, nor for the power exerted by places and by experience itself. While the gaze mediates experience, so experience—especially in the case of a receptive and "visionary" architect—can transform the gaze. Although architects typically go to places to confirm and augment what they know from drawings and photographs, the physical encounter with the "other" has thus had a more explosive effect at times. Indeed, the "shock of the real" is familiar enough to most travelers, and not just architects: firsthand experience of a canonical building often turns out to be very different from what one anticipated from the images, the media, the history books. In this way, "reality," even if not a stable category itself, modifies or offers resistance to the predispositions of the gaze. It is worth noting that Foucault himself, specifically in his late work on sexuality, acknowledged the reciprocity between the gaze and experience, affirming the transfigurative potential of the latter: "Man is an animal of experience," he writes. "He is involved *ad infinitum* within a process that, by defining a field of objects, at the same time changes him, deforms him, transforms him, and transfigures him as a subject."[9]

The following pages chart the experiences of five twentieth-century architects for whom tourism both had a transforming impact on their way of seeing and led to seminal new

ideas about architecture and the world. While travel was important for many if not most modern architects—some of whom experienced its effects more as a result of exile or emigration than by choice—the figures considered here are exceptional in terms of the thematic relationship between their activity as tourists and their theory and practice. Their respective destinations and preferred modes of representation are connected with a way of visioning and envisioning architecture at a particular moment in time. In each case, as we shall see, the architect's gaze came to focus on one or more privileged "sites of seeing" and found expression through a preferred strategy of description. In each case, the architect succeeded in converting his or her experience into an original form of critical reflection and, ultimately, architectural production. Finally, in each case, both the discursive context and the innovative outcome of the architect's encounter with the chosen site are bound up with the evolution of the twentieth-century architectural imagination.

VOYAGE/*VOYANT*

Le Corbusier's *Voyage d'Orient* is the travelogue of a journey to "the East" taken in 1911 by the twenty-four-year-old Swiss architect then known as Charles-Edouard Jeanneret. At the time working in the office of Peter Behrens, the young Jeanneret set out from Berlin with his knapsack and one companion, a Flemish art history student named Auguste Klipstein. They traveled for six months by second-class ship and rail, on donkey, cart, and foot, from Dresden by way of Prague, Vienna, and the Balkans to Adrianople (Edirne in northwest Turkey) and Istanbul, then across the Sea of Marmora to Bursa in Asia Minor, and back by the southern route, Greece (Athos and Athens) and Italy (Naples, Pompeii, Rome, Florence, Pisa). They consumed cheap wine, endured the discomfort of bedbugs, and waxed poetic about beauty, from vernacular buildings and sublime landscapes to clay pots and the native dress of women. Turkish girls in burkas excited the young Jeanneret's exotic-erotic gaze; he imagined them to be coquettishly flirting with him underneath their mysterious veils. Above all, it was "the irresistible pull of the Mediterranean," "the persistent call of the sun, the wide expanses of blue seas, and the great white walls of temples," that led him from the "gossamer architecture" of the chilly north to the more plastic formal worlds of Turkey, Greece, and southern Italy.[10] He envisaged the experience as "an ideally shaped vase" from which would flow "the heart's most profound feelings."

Far from the deluxe Grand Tour of his forebear Robert Adam, Jeanneret's self-educating mission was at least as grandiose. "I open my eyes very wide, taking in all around me [through] my myopic eyes behind my glasses—these sorry spectacles that bestow upon me a doctoral air or the look of a clergyman."[12] The near-sighted architect thus absorbed "the spectacle of things."[13] He sketched incessantly, captured his impressions in watercolor, took photographs with a new camera he had purchased for the trip, and effusively confided his observations to his travel diary. In addition to the diary, he produced nearly three hundred drawings, five hundred photographs, and six *carnets* during his half year on the road. As on an earlier trip to Italy in 1907 when he had steeped himself in travel literature from Hippolyte Taine to John Ruskin, he prepared carefully for the voyage, filling his knapsack with Baedeker guidebooks and, especially for the Balkan part of his itinerary,

relying on the counsel of a personal mentor, the Swiss writer and aesthete William Ritter. His arrival at the Acropolis, deliberately saved for the return leg, was, not surprisingly, a climactic moment overdetermined by all those who had preceded him. Yet if—as Stanislaus von Moos has elaborated in a recent exhibition catalogue—the architect embarked with a set of stock conceptions and expectations,[14] his voyage was also an exhilarating adventure of discovery and self-discovery, not lacking in improvised detours, unexpected encounters, and spontaneous revelations. His diary is filled with a young man's *esprit de route* as it also reflects a voracious and quite open-minded curiosity about different cultures and struggles to articulate new sensations and ideas. Landscapes, people, and vernacular constructions proved as interesting to him as monumental buildings. While the voyage confirmed his conviction of the power of classical architecture and platonic forms, as epitomized by the Parthenon, it also awakened in him a more haptic appreciation of the role of light and landscape in the experience and animation of space.

Predictably Jeanneret invokes the trope of the traveler versus the tourist. "How painful it is to meet tourists!" he jots down in his diary, later returning to dilate:

> They are philistines in exodus, noticed more than ever because they are outside their milieu and stand out. You see them, but especially you hear them because their footsteps are as confident as their taste, and they stride along their art pilgrimages proclaiming oracles. Never is their admiration for the artist's ideas. Paste and imitation gold thrills as intensely as ever.... The public doesn't know anything anymore; it has lost a sense of proportion.[15]

If the evocation of philistines on art pilgrimages registers the realities of an emergent mass tourism as it anticipates the "Bilbao effect" of nearly a century later, Jeanneret's language also partakes of an elitist and Nietzschean current prevalent in European cultural circles during the years before World War I. He continues in the same passage:

> I place all my hopes in those who, having started from the beginning, are already well advanced and know much.... Purification is a vital necessity.... [W]e shall return, yes, to the health that belongs to this epoch...and then from there to beauty. Throughout the world, we *are returning;* the scales are falling from our eyes. The infectious germ will be opposed by a youthful, vigorous, joyous germ born of the need "to conquer or to die."

Underneath this overheated rhetoric of purification and conquest, however, we may also discern the opening notes of Le Corbusier's life-long polemic against "eyes that do not see," a theme to become the leitmotif of *Vers une architecture* (1923) and the architect's subsequent philosophy of architectural creation. Only those artists and architects who instinctively knew how to "take possession of space," to "occupy" it and thereby fathom its hidden dimensions, were vouchsafed, in Le Corbusier's view, the consummatory and ineffable experience of "plastic emotion."[16] In this sense, while his trip falls into the lineage of both the Grand Tour and the romantic nineteenth-century journey, it also has affinities

Charles-Edouard Jeanneret [Le Corbusier], sketches of pottery from the Balkans, 1911.

Charles-Edouard Jeanneret, sketch of the Seraglio, Istanbul, 1911. © 2005 Artists Rights Society (ARS), New York/ADAGP, Paris/FLC

with the more visionary and ecstatic tradition of the French *poètes maudits*, avant-garde "seers" like Rimbaud and Mallarmé who ventured into "the unknown" in order to transcend a vulgar and etiolated bourgeois culture and to make themselves "absolutely modern."[17]

For Le Corbusier, the route from the nineteenth century into modernity thus paradoxically led through antiquity and folkloric destinations. A decade and a half later, he would sum up the twofold architectural lesson of his 1911 trip in a concluding autobiographical "confession" appended to *Les Arts décoratifs d'aujourd'hui* (1925), a polemical book in which he enunciated his critique of decoration and his concept of the *objet-type* in arguments indebted in part to Adolf Loos. "An emotional response is provoked [in the traveler] by a complex of forms assembled in a precise relationship: horizontals and verticals," he writes. "Or else it is the work which by the progressive distillation of folk cultures reveals to us a type-thought, potentially universal, the language of the heart of mankind."[18]

As to his eagerly anticipated encounter with the Acropolis, the architect could hardly bear, when he at last arrived there, to confront it in all its "harsh poetry," its "ineluctable presence." After delaying the moment so as to make his approach at the recommended hour of sundown, he ended up spending five weeks communing with the ruins in the most direct possible way. Lying flat on his stomach under the blazing Athens sun, he examined the Propylaea's foundations, calibrating the dimensions of its shafts with his own body—a measuring method he would translate a few decades later into a proportional system of his own devising, the Modulor. Finally, having passed through this self-imposed ascetic ordeal,

he took leave of his "chilling dialogues with silent stones" confirmed in his vocation as an architect: "I left the Acropolis burdened by a heavy premonition, not daring to imagine that one day I would have to create."[19]

We may note that the passage cited earlier about purification—to which Le Corbusier retrospectively accorded importance, to judge by the fact that he reprinted it (slightly modified) in his concluding confession in *Les Arts décoratifs d'aujourd'hui*—appears late in the 1911 diary in a chapter entitled "A Jumble of Recollections and Regrets," and is somewhat exceptional. Despite an awkwardly self-conscious literariness throughout, Jeanneret's tone in *Voyage* is generally more anecdotal and impressionistic than theoretical or polemical, oscillating between light-hearted narration and flights of emotion. This is not surprising in light of the fact that he wrote the diary with the intent of serializing parts in the local Swiss newspaper *La Feuille d'Avis de La Chaux-de-Fonds* while he was still traveling, having negotiated the fee of one sou per line before his departure. After his return he made at least two unsuccessful attempts to get the manuscript published in book form. Half a century later, in 1965, he would return to it again, reediting it a month before his death. Thus his early travel diary became his final published work, appearing for the first time in full posthumously in 1966.

In fact, however, Le Corbusier would repeatedly return to the memories and images of his "decisive" youthful journey throughout his career. Sometimes misdated and often recontextualized, his drawings reappear in many of his publications, including, besides the book on the decorative arts, his other polemical statements of the 1920s, *Vers une architecture, Almanach d'architecture moderne,* and *Urbanisme.* And while writing, photography, and drawing would all figure centrally in his construction of his public persona, it was this last that served him throughout his career, not just as a way of conveying his architectural ideas to the world but as a deeply personal vehicle of

Center, Le Corbusier, sculptural ensemble of rooftop of Unite d'Habitation, Marseille. © 2005 Artists Rights Society (ARS), New York/ADAGP, Paris/FLC

Charles-Edouard Jeanneret standing next to a column of the Parthenon in 1911. From the chapter "Sur l'Acropole," *Almanach d'architecture moderne* (1926)

discovery. The drawing became the plane of intersection between the world as found and its transformation into his own vision. As he would later write in an often-quoted passage from *Creation Is a Patient Search:*

> When one travels and works with visual things—architecture, painting or sculpture—one uses one's eyes and *draws,* so as to fix deep down in one's experience what is seen. Once the impression has been recorded by the pencil, it stays for good, entered, registered, inscribed. The camera is a tool for idlers, who use a machine to do their *seeing* for them. To draw oneself, to trace the lines, handle the volumes, organize the surface...all this means first to look, and then to observe and finally perhaps to discover...and it is then that inspiration may come. Inventing, creating, one's whole being is drawn into action, and it is this action which counts. *Others* stood indifferent—but *you saw!*[20]

As the most active way of apprehending the world—of overcoming the passivity of purely spectatorial seeing—drawing for Le Corbusier was the first step in a "spongelike" absorption of what was around him and an essential psychological and technical stage in the process of creation.[21] To see actively was to draw and to draw was to possess. "Taking possession of space is the first gesture of living things...," he declares in his credo "L'Espace indicible," in which, not by chance, metaphors of possession, occupation, acquisition, and control recur, as we have suggested above.

In turn, it was precisely this "possessive" vision that emboldened Le Corbusier to project his way of seeing onto the world. This had other consequences in his mature career. Recent scholars have emphasized, not without justice, the architect's territorializing gaze.[22] Yet the extensive drawn and written record of his travels that he would continue to produce over the course of his career provides evidence of a profound reciprocity between his gaze and his experience. His next significant travel document was a book entitled *Précisions sur un état présent de l'architecture et de l'urbanisme,* the fruit of a three-month trip to South America—Argentina, Brazil, and Uruguay—in late 1929. Unlike the earlier book, a product of his formative years, this one was, quite literally, a master narrative. The architect transcribed for posterity ten lectures that he delivered in Buenos Aires, presumably to grateful audiences, in which he expounded his theories of architecture, urbanism, technology, dwelling, and domestic equipment, with specific application to the case of South America. Foreshadowing Koolhaas in China, the architect took note of the nascent urban tensions in São Paulo, Montevideo, and Rio de Janeiro unleashed by these cities' precipitous growth, and presented himself with European hubris as nothing less than savior-conquistador: "One would not have gone so far to give lectures on architecture and urbanism," he declares in his foreword, "if one did not feel himself in a position to impart certain necessary realities."[23]

At the same time, in the book's "Prologue Américain" and concluding "Corollaire Brésilien," he expressed his exhilaration at discovering the sensuous and spectacular geography of the South American continent—its meandering rivers, fecund plains, grandiose mountains, and boundless horizons, as revealed, above all, from the window of an airplane. It was this experience of the landscape, which he again recorded in sketches and prose, as well as in

another privileged mode, didactic diagrams, that would engender a shift in his work from the abstract, white, and mechanistic rationalism of the 1920s toward the more organic and regionally inflected projects of the 1930s, starting with the Errazuris and de Mandrot houses for Chile and the south of France, respectively. The early appreciation of regional and vernacular building that Le Corbusier forged on his 1911 trip thus had its delayed effect. He would elaborate this vision most extensively during the 1930s in his succession of schemes for Algiers. In the many drawings with which he filled his Algerian notebooks, the sinuosity of the curved line serves to describe the lyrical Mediterranean topography into which he inserted his monumental "Obus" skyscraper as it also does, at an altogether different scale, the recumbent bodies of odalisque-like women encountered in the casbah.

In contrast, a book written after a trip made in 1935 to the United States, *When the Cathedrals Were White,* subtitled *A Journey to the Country of the Timid People,* reflects an architectural gaze colored by preconceptions of another kind. If Le Corbusier's voyages to the East and South were filtered through colonial and orientalizing fantasies, on the one hand, and neoplatonic idealism, on the other, his love-hate account of the "fairy catastrophe" of New York was refracted through the lens of the anticapitalist criticism rampant at this date in Europe, especially France. With monumental arrogance and a taste for publicity, the Parisian architect proclaimed Manhattan's skyscrapers "too small" because they failed to submit to any overarching urban discipline or rational plan. Yet this experience too would have its impact on the architect's way of seeing.[24]

"Le Corbusier Scans Gotham's Towers." *New York Times,* November 3, 1935. NYT Pictures, © 1935 The New York Times Co.

CAMERA EYE

For early twentieth-century European visitors like Le Corbusier, the meaning of "America" was both thrilling and threatening. The United States appeared at once the privileged locus of modernity and the dream-nightmare destiny of Europe; it filled the role—as Jean-Louis Cohen and Hubert Damisch have suggested in another exhibition and catalogue related to the theme of the architect-tourist—of "Europe's unconscious."[25] But it was a scene with which any architect of modern sensibility had to reckon. As Gertrude Stein wrote in 1928, "America is just now the oldest country in the world" because "it is she who is the mother of the twentieth century civilization."[26]

Another modern site/sightseer for whom the North American metropolis was an object of desire and foreboding was the German architect Erich Mendelsohn, who made his first trip to New York a decade before Le Corbusier. Mendelsohn traveled across the Atlantic at the behest of his client and patron Rudolf Mosse, who commissioned him to write a column of "American Notes" for Mosse's Berlin newspaper, the *Tageblatt.* He sailed to New York in 1924. His shipboard companion was the filmmaker Fritz Lang, and for Lang, out of this trip and a first view of the lights and buildings of Manhattan seen from a boat quarantined on the West Side docks, came the inspiration for the 1927 film *Metropolis.* Mendelsohn's own view was no less expressionistic. Among the most original books in the library of architectural modernism are two volumes reflecting his travel experience: *Amerika: Bilderbuch eines Architekton* (1926; second edition, 1928) and *Russland Europa Amerika: Ein architektonischer Querschnitt* (1929). If for Le Corbusier drawing remained the privileged instrument for assimilating the experience of places, for Mendelsohn, at least in these two books, it was the camera. Indeed, while Mendelsohn was Le Corbusier's equal as a master of the freehand drawing and made numerous sketches during his American travels, it was the album of photographs, organized as a vividly cinematographic sequence of images, that served to translate his vision of America's power, dynamism, and mechanistic ambiance.

The required Grand Tour now led from Manhattan to Chicago, Buffalo, Detroit, and Pittsburgh. By the time of Mendelsohn's trip, images and reports on American grain elevators, factories, and skyscrapers had been circulating in Germany for at least a decade, and certainly these prepared his reception of them. But it was the German architect's radically subjective interpretation of the awesome American urban and industrial landscape that most distinguished his two books. As Cohen points out in an extensive analysis of the 1926 publication, the oversized vertical format, wide margins, heliogravure technique, and notational text made a bold break with traditional iconographic treatments, which had tended to alternate panoramic views with building close-ups and standard narrative descriptions.[27] Mendelsohn, who took about half the photographs in the book himself, favored a low-angle, often vertiginously tipped shot. Not coincidentally, this innovation was much admired by Soviet Constructivist architects. "A first leafing through its pages thrills us like a dramatic film," wrote El Lissitzky. "In order to understand some of the photographs you must lift the book over your head and rotate it."[28] Alexander Rodchenko, published an article in *Novy LEF* juxtaposing two images from Mendelsohn's book with conventional photographs of the same subjects.

Opposite, Front covers of Erich Mendelsohn's *Amerika: Bilderbuch eines Architekten* (1926) and *Russland Europa Amerika: Ein architektonischer Querschnitt* (1929). Cover designs by Mendelsohn.

Left, A back street in Chicago. Photo: Erich Mendelsohn. From *Amerika: Bilderbuch eines Architekten*. The caption reads, "Alleys, passageways 5 meters wide separating walls 100 meters high. The reverse side of the gleaming facades along the lake. Damp, dark and nevertheless people's escape routes. All the fire escapes empty into them."

Bottom, Seventh Avenue, New York. Photo: Erich Mendelsohn. From *Amerika: Bilderbuch eines Architekten*. The caption reads, "Finally new knowledge. The bold step of consciously transferring the unconscious objectivity of rear facades to the entire structure. Thus turning it over to the aesthetic sensibilities of the main street, to pampered eyes and brains loaded down with tradition. With the breadth of mind and purposefulness of its face, it overcomes the confusion of the street, the chaos of the ads—for the first time."

Mendelsohn's expressionistic upward gaze also contrasted with the God's-eye or airplane view preferred by Le Corbusier. The view from below emphasized the gigantism of the skyscraping buildings and the city's accumulating congestion. The metaphor of "huddled masses yearning to breathe free" might literally describe the aspirations of New York's looming architecture seen through the German architect's lens, as it also expressed the contradictions between technological and social progress that Mendelsohn was bent on exposing in the capitalist metropolis. The architect frequently focuses on infrastructural and unfinished elements in the high-rise city, dramatizing its condition of being ceaselessly under construction. The camera also tends to freeze on residual and ephemeral details, especially advertising images. In a shot of the rear facade of the Tuller Hotel in Detroit (a photograph taken not by Mendelsohn himself but by the Danish architect Knud Lonberg-Holm, who supplied Mendelsohn with a number of striking views in the book), one sees posters for the Ringling Brothers circus plastered on a bare brick wall. Images like these and Mendelsohn's accompanying comments call to mind Thorstein Veblen's disparaging remark that the back sides of American buildings were preferable to their overembellished fronts.[29] Mendelsohn's photographic point of view likewise gives literal representation to a definition that Guy Debord was to coin in *The Society of the Spectacle* half a century later: the spectacle is capital, in Debord's axiom, accumulated to the point it becomes image.[30]

Mendelsohn would continue to work through his ambivalence with respect to the system responsible for producing the American metropolis even more explicitly in his second book. Subtitled *An Architectural Cross-Section,* it deploys the technique of montage in even more literal fashion. The architect intercuts full-page images of both positive and negative examples of American, Russian, and European architecture, presenting a dialectical argument in which Europe is positioned between the two diametric world models, U.S. and U.S.S.R. While America appears as the frontier of concretized industrial advancement and brute—brutal—materialism, the still largely rural, technologically backward Soviet Union, to which Mendelsohn made three trips in 1925–26 in connection with a commission for a textile factory in Leningrad, is portrayed as the homeland of mystical spirituality, from fantastic onion-domed churches to utopian dream projects by the young Ivan Leonidov (the latter criticized as being paper-architecture clichés). Mendelsohn thus made a graphic argument that it was the task of the European architect to mediate between the poles of reality and dreams, material and spirit. He offered an example of this Hegelian synthesis in one of the final images in the book, a model of his own factory in Leningrad; here, he noted, rational spatial analysis harmoniously resolved the competing technical and social demands of the modern industrial complex.

Times Square (Broadway and 48th Street), New York, at night. Photo: Fritz Lang. From *Amerika: Bilderbuch eines Architekten.* Mendelsohn's caption reads, "Uncanny. The contours of the buildings are erased. But in one's unconscious they still rise, chase one another, trample one another. This is the foil for the flaming scripts, the rocket fire of moving illuminated ads, emerging and submerging, disappearing and breaking out again over the thousands of autos and the maelstrom of pleasure-seeking people. Still disordered, because exaggerated, but all the same already full of imaginative beauty, which will one day be complete."

Erich Mendelsohn, Deukonhaus, Berlin, 1927. Photo: Arthur Köster

Yet if Mendelsohn remained conflicted or indeed negative in both these books in his attitude toward the profit-driven world of American capitalism, in the second half of the 1920s he was to exploit the potential of illuminated signage and *Reklamearchitektur*—advertising architecture—to spectacular advantage in his own work. In projects for department stores, movie theaters, and press offices, he celebrated the literally electrifying energy of the new metropolis while disciplining the anarchy of Times Square to the more controlled context of the European city.

Mendelsohn's spark of invention was soon to flicker, however. Forced by the rise of National Socialism to emigrate in the 1930s first to England and then to Palestine, he ended up during World War II in the United States, ultimately settling in San Francisco and thus reaching the western terminus of the journey he began in New York harbor two decades earlier. But the critical spirit and creative tensions that had animated his European work of the 1920s, years when the dream of America so vividly haunted the imagination of the avant-garde tourist, were now gone. Once "at home" in California, Mendelsohn's architecture no longer embodied the dialectics of *Amerikanismus* but became rather blandly American.

IN SEARCH OF AN "OTHER" ARCHITECTURE

The cataclysm of World War II brought not just a sense of the enervation of traditional European culture and the triumphal expansion of American civilization but a deep crisis of confidence in Western rationalism. With the unleashing of struggles for decolonization in Third World countries, the imagination of certain members of the next generation of architects began to stray in different directions.

For the Dutch architect Aldo van Eyck, the search for existential meaning and an authentic form of urban life transcending Western history led to sub-Saharan Africa. Van Eyck's initial inspiration for his series of trips to the African continent came from his reading during the war years of an account by the anthropologist Marcel Griaule of the 1931–33 Dakar-Djibouti mission to the Dogon, famously published in the Surrealist journal *Minotaure*.[31] Van Eyck made expeditions to North Africa and the oases of the central Sahara in 1950–52, but to his regret was unable to travel beyond the Hoggar Mountains in Algeria. He returned to the African continent in early 1960, on this occasion journeying inland from the west coast by way of the Niger River to reach the remote Dogon region located south of Timbuktu in Mali. There he spent five weeks studying and photographing this still virtually intact indigenous culture.[32]

Van Eyck intended to collect his reflections and photographs of the Dogon experience in a book but he never got around to it. Instead, he published substantial expositions in 1968 in the first issue of the University of Pennsylvania school of architecture student journal, *VIA,* a special number dedicated to ecology in design, and the following year in the volume *Meaning in Architecture,* a collection of essays edited by George Baird and Charles Jencks, reflecting the then-current architectural vogue for structuralism and semiology.[33] In the latter volume Van Eyck's presentation occupies forty pages and includes contributions by two Swiss anthropologists, pioneers in the new field of ethnopsychoanalysis, whom Van Eyck met and

A shrine in the Dogon village of Ogol, 1960. Photo: Aldo van Eyck

befriended in the village of Ogol where they were carrying out studies on the Dogon personality.

Like Le Corbusier's voyage to the East, Van Eyck's journey was a quest for meaning and form beyond the bounds of European civilization. Rather than history, however, his gaze partook of anthropology. This to some extent gave social-scientific underpinnings to what was fundamentally a poetic project. Van Eyck's texts, diagrams, and richly saturated black-and-white photographs, taken with a square-format camera, capture both the timelessness and the quotidianity of the Dogon buildings, objects, ceremonies, and landscapes. The camera alternates between an aestheticizing and a documentary approach: on the one hand, it abstracts the timeless formal qualities of the Dogon built environment; on the other, it frames the exotic inhabitants with ethnological curiosity, although without spectacularizing them. The inhabitants reciprocate the photographer's gaze with a certain bemusement or nonchalance, tolerating him but maintaining their distance.

The turmoil that roiled many African nations in the 1950s did not affect the peaceable Dogon, but it is worth noting that Mali liberated itself from French rule in 1960, the year of Van Eyck's visit. With respect to anthropology, decolonization struggles spurred interest among Western intellectuals in developing nonexploitative ways of studying native cultures. The book *Tristes Tropiques* appeared in 1955, an account by the Belgian-born anthropologist Claude Lévi-Strauss of his expedition to the Amerindian tribes in the interior of Brazil. Lévi-Strauss's humanistic structuralism centered on the idea of universal mythic structures; these structures not only were shared by all cultures, whether civilized or "savage," he argued, but were based on binary oppositions that the myths were designed to reconcile. Van Eyck's library in the 1950s included, besides the writings of Marcel Griaule, classic anthropological texts by Franz Boas and Margaret Mead, among others; apparently he did not read Lévi-Strauss until the mid–1960s.[34] Nonetheless, his thinking has affinities with the emerging discipline of structural anthropology, most especially in terms of his universalist conception of architecture as a symbolic structure within which oppositions could be elaborated and reconciled.

Postcolonial discourse also engendered a resurgence of aesthetic interest in non-Western and indigenous cultures. During the early postwar years Van Eyck was close to the artists of the CoBrA group, and on his trip to North Africa in 1951 he was accompanied by the CoBrA painter Corneille. The Surrealist-influenced group's engagement with neoprimitivist as well as ludic aesthetics reinforced Van Eyck's own preoccupation with these themes. In addition to designing several CoBrA installations during these years, he constructed a series of playgrounds for the city of Amsterdam, devising variations on simple geometric arrangements evocative of the spirit of child's play. More polemically, Van Eyck had been an outspoken advocate ever since the war of "imagination" in architecture. This he saw as an essential corrective to the reductive and mechanistic thinking of the first generation of modernism, represented by the International Congresses of Modern Architecture (CIAM). Under this banner Van Eyck would become one of the instigators of the breakaway Team

A Dogon man, 1960. Photo: Aldo van Eyck

10 group, calling in the 1950s for more humanistic and "associational" patterns of inhabitation and urban settlement. The collective housing designed by Candilis, Josic and Woods in North Africa, admirably variegated in terms of its public and private spaces, and introduced at CIAM's ninth meeting in Aix-en-Provence in 1953, was a rallying point for Team 10's formation. At the same meeting in Aix, the report of the commission on "Aesthetics and the Human Habitat," which Van Eyck was instrumental in drafting, declared, "A Cameroon hut has more dignity than most primitive houses," continuing:

> Primitive architecture, when approached fairly, can be seen as a symbol that directly reflects a way of life which has come down through the ages, and which has roots that penetrate deeply into human and cosmic conditions. Modern painters, for the last forty years, have been demonstrating to us that primitive and prehistoric art can help us to rediscover more direct means of expression. In the same way primitive architecture can give a new depth to contemporary architecture that can enable it to meet urgent challenges of today.[35]

In 1955–60 Van Eyck designed his most important built work, the Amsterdam Children's Home. Here the African imaginary found abstracted formal expression in the rounded hillocks of the roof, evocative of a desert sandscape; in the additive, nonhierarchical plan composition, replicating the interwoven communal organization and "doorstep philosophy" Van Eyck would so admire in the Dogon village; and in the sensitive scaling of spaces, reflecting a child's view of the world at different developmental stages. He would present this project at CIAM's final meeting, which took place in Otterlo in 1959, an event for which he also prepared a special issue of the Dutch journal *Forum* entitled "The Story of Another Idea." That publication featured photographs of African village scenes juxtaposed with images of everyday street life in Western cities, concluding with two images of the North African vernacular alongside the slogan "Vers une 'casbah' organisée"[36]—a challenge to Le Corbusier's rationalist urbanism but perhaps also a salute across the generation to the older architect's own Algerian experience.

Aldo van Eyck, Children's Home, Amsterdam, 1955–60. Photo: Aldo van Eyck

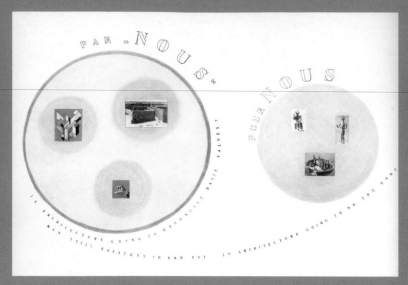

"Is architecture going to reconcile basic values?" Diagram by Aldo van Eyck, published in *New Frontiers in Architecture: CIAM '59 in Otterlo* (1961).

Inasmuch as Van Eyck's attitude toward the Dogon was already largely formed prior to his trip, his encounter in 1960 served more to confirm and deepen than alter his ideas. To the fundamental question he posed during the postwar period, of whether architecture was still capable of reconciling basic human values, the unalienated Dogon culture, as seen through his rather roseate glasses, became a utopian—or, more precisely, heterotopian—answer, a "counterform," as he put it. The Dogon settlements, their everyday objects like baskets, their functional spaces like granaries, their ritual observances all revealed a "miraculous" reciprocity between the macrocosmic world and the microcosmic: the Dogon house was like a small city, the Dogon village like a large house. A year after his trip to Mali, Van Eyck would undertake a similar immersion in the Pueblo culture of New Mexico, there finding further corroboration for such idiosyncratically Van Eyckian concepts as twinphenomena, labyrinthian clarity, right-size, and spiritual equipoise. In an unpublished manuscript entitled *The Child, the City, and the Architect* written shortly afterward, Van Eyck deplored the advancing culture of mass tourism and its commodified gaze:

> It requires far more to appreciate a wide world than a limited one—beyond mere sensation and novelty, which is all that is reaped when people have themselves transported unprepared from place to place round the globe. Today the number of places in the world that are not yet encompassed by the vicious circle of profit and boredom—appeasing sensation—is growing smaller as the cruel fingers of comfort penetrate the more inhospitable regions, paving the way for unsatiable herds [*sic*].... The tragedy of it is that instead of carrying back the spiritual substance with which to enrich their own mind and the society to which they belong, they graft the horrors of their own onto those they gape at, in order to do so comfortably accommodated. Since, furthermore, the last remnants of collective dignity are to be found among people whose livelihood is precarious, the disintegrating ruthlessness of those who thus trespass, imparting nothing but what is exploitable for their own sake, undermines that which, if encountered with care, humility, and real understanding, would not only prove to be of inestimable value, but would develop positively through contact.[37]

In light of this critique, an exhibition curated by the Viennese emigré architect Bernard Rudofsky that opened at the Museum of Modern Art in New York in late 1964, entitled *Architecture without Architects,* offers a pertinent contrast. If by virtue of his relatively circumscribed production Van Eyck's writing and architecture had a limited reception, not penetrating far outside the architectural milieu of CIAM, the Dutch scene, and an admiring circle of students, Rudofsky's enormously popular exhibition, which traveled to eighty-four venues over eleven years and was accompanied by a vivid catalogue, had much broader impact. It was focused on indigenous built structures around the world, or what Rudofsky called "non-pedigreed architecture." Consisting entirely of black-and-white photographs, usually one to a locale, and mounted on a lightweight frame-and-panel structure designed for portability, the installation offered a seductively abstract and immersive total environment.[38]

Like Van Eyck, Rudofsky was an avid tourist over many years. Also like the Dutch architect, he was interested in identifying commonalities among different forms of human shelter and, more polemically, in countering "the narrow world of official and commercial architecture."[39] But his gaze was more a glance or glimpse. This even the jacket copy of the catalogue made explicit: "By avoiding the geographical and social prejudices that have obscured what [Rudofsky] views as a *total* picture of architecture, he offers us glimpses of worlds that were hitherto unknown and, indeed, unsuspected." If what Van Eyck was after in Mali and New Mexico may be characterized as "thick description," then, to use the anthropologist Clifford Geertz's term, what Rudofsky succeeded in producing with his site-bite approach was decidedly "thin." Nonetheless the architect's seductive selection of images struck a resonant chord in the mid–1960s, a moment when the late-modernist architectural establishment was in crisis, political and institutional authority was under siege from the Left, and many were setting out or dropping out in pursuit of countercultural lifestyles with little more than a backpack.

Of the 125 or so photographs published in the catalogue, a small number were actually taken by Rudofsky himself over his forty years of travel. The rest were culled from a wide variety of sources, including natural history archives, anthropology museums, press and information services, *National Geographic* magazine, travel agencies, and a handful of architectural photographers. They are organized according to a taxonomy of categories like "model hill towns," "quasi-sacral architecture," "primeval forms," and "nomadic architecture" and accompanied by extended captions. Interspersed among the decontextualized images are a handful of schematic maps and historical views, but no plans or architectural drawings. The categoric rubrics allow remote built environments to be juxtaposed by virtue of superficial formal similarities: a castle near Madrid appears on a page with one in west Pakistan, a church carved out of rock in the Gironde in France with one in Abyssinia. Also recycled are Marcel Griaule's photographs of the Dogon.

This is not the critical montage of Mendelsohn, nor is it a matter of serious cross-cultural or typological analysis. In its universalizing categories it projects an idealistic belief (not

coincidentally at a moment of escalating war in Vietnam and racial strife in the United States) in similarities among the world's peoples as demonstrated by the shared formal traits of their functional and symbolic constructions. In this respect it recalls MoMA's earlier *Family of Man* exhibition (1955), another ideologically loaded event proffering a sentimental vision of "one world" at the height of the Cold War. It also bears resemblance to the pop-anthropological worldview announced at this time by Marshall McLuhan in *The Gutenberg Galaxy:* that of the global village. In McLuhan's optimistic media theory, the instantaneous image-world engendered by the new electronic communications was destined to bring the planet's far-flung peoples closer together around the surrogate hearth of the television set. Similarly, *Architecture without Architects* was designed to present the "whole earth" to itself within the unifying framework and constructed immediacy of a touring exhibition. As McLuhan would write in a subsequent book, "Remote folklore, remote societies are being abstracted from their matrix and enlarged by microscopic vision.... The anthropologist is a connoisseur of cultures as art forms."[40]

LEARNING BY GOING

We have made a detour to Rudofsky primarily to contrast his way of seeing to Van Eyck's. More consequential for the vicissitudes of twentieth-century architectural thought was the tourist experience of another architect, Robert Venturi, together with his partner and wife, Denise Scott Brown. In fall 1968, Venturi and Scott Brown along with their associate Steven Izenour and a studio of nine Yale architecture students made a field trip to a location almost as exotic as the Dogon, at least for a group of Ivy League academics: Las Vegas. This may have been among the earliest instances of the long-distance studio trips that have today become a staple and indeed almost an entitlement within elite professional architecture programs. But it falls well within the tradition of the Grand Tour, which Robert Venturi had himself undertaken in 1948 after his first year of graduate architecture study at Princeton—a school still oriented to the system of Beaux-Arts education—and again in 1954–56 as a winner of the Prix de Rome.

These early travels, and particularly Venturi's experience of the baroque and mannerist architecture of Rome, would have a profound influence on his first book, the "gentle manifesto" *Complexity and Contradiction in Architecture,* published in 1966 by the Museum of Modern Art. The presentation of postage-stamp-size photographs and architectural drawings of an eclectic assortment of buildings, many of which Venturi visited on his two trips, has been compared to a slide lecture. It is perhaps equally reminiscent of a travel album. Either way, the images provide pictorial evidence to support the Philadelphia architect's case for an inclusive and heterodox language of architectural form.

Scott Brown, for her part, had also traveled widely after leaving her native South Africa to continue her architectural education in London and then, following a period of practice with her first husband in London, Rome, and back in South Africa, at the University of Pennsylvania, where she met Venturi in 1960. Five years later, en route to a teaching job in California, she drove across the United States, visiting several Western cities, including

Las Vegas. She returned to Las Vegas in 1966 with Venturi. The trip was a revelation for both: "Dazed by the desert sun and dazzled by the signs, both loving and hating what we saw," she recalled, "we were jolted clear out of our aesthetic skins."[41] This experience led to a first publication of their Las Vegas thesis in March 1968 in Architectural Forum, "A Significance for A&P Parking Lots or Learning from Las Vegas," and the semester afterward to the Yale studio trip. A lavish, large-format book filled with striking graphics and extensive documentation of the project, including press clippings ("Yale University Study Of Las Vegas Could Alter The City's View of Itself"), followed in 1972.[42]

It was no accident, of course, that the paradigm of "learning from" should emanate from an academic context given the Venturis' strong pedagogical involvements in these years. Their field study harks back to twentieth-century theories of progressive education from John Dewey to the Bauhaus, except with a touristic variation on the action philosophy of "learning by doing." It also draws on the methods of empirical sociology, which Scott Brown had absorbed from Herbert Gans and her other teachers of urban planning at Penn, and which now served to inflect Venturi's strictly formalist approach in his earlier book. There was also an implicit connection back to Le Corbusier's "Lesson of Rome" in *Vers une architecture*—Le Corbusier's didacticism likewise ironic in light of his antiacademic polemic—and a debt as well to Scott Brown's academic mentors at the Architectural Association in London, Peter and Alison Smithson. The Smithsons' manifesto "But Today

Robert Venturi and Denise Scott Brown in Las Vegas, 1966. Courtesy of Venturi, Scott Brown & Associates

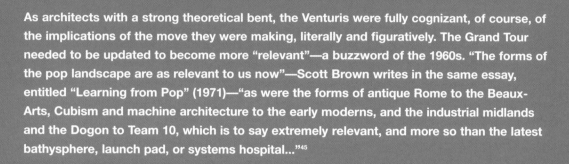

We Collect Ads" (1956) was an injunction to reinvigorate an exhausted high-culture architecture by inoculating it with the energies of mass culture and advertising: "Ordinary life is receiving powerful impulses from a new source.... We must somehow get the measure of this intervention if we want to match its powerful and exciting impulses with our own."[43] In turn, Scott Brown would write of Las Vegas: "New sources are sought when the old forms go stale."[44]

As architects with a strong theoretical bent, the Venturis were fully cognizant, of course, of the implications of the move they were making, literally and figuratively. The Grand Tour needed to be updated to become more "relevant"—a buzzword of the 1960s. "The forms of the pop landscape are as relevant to us now"—Scott Brown writes in the same essay, entitled "Learning from Pop" (1971)—"as were the forms of antique Rome to the Beaux-Arts, Cubism and machine architecture to the early moderns, and the industrial midlands and the Dogon to Team 10, which is to say extremely relevant, and more so than the latest bathysphere, launch pad, or systems hospital..."[45]

This was obviously a jab from the camp of "realism" at paper architects like Archigram and technofuturists like Reyner Banham. But apart from an affirmation of the realities of consumer culture in everyday American life, what exactly was there for architects to learn from Las Vegas in the context of the stated purpose of the studio, namely, "formal analysis as design research"? Or for that matter, from Levittown, the subject of another Yale "learning from" studio taught by the Venturi team the following year? Indeed, this was the central contradiction (and not in the sense of Venturi's earlier book) of the Ivy League slumming. Not only were formal lessons to be derived from a study of the most unformal or informal place in the world—an oxymoron anticipating Koolhaas's Lagos project—but the lower depths of American commercial culture were to be plumbed through the lens and methodology of high-academic "analysis" and "research." It is important to emphasize that, in line with this formalist-rationalist-modernist project, the Venturis never set out to surrender to the object of their gaze, but rather endeavored to maintain their sense of critical objectivity or, probably better described, critical receptivity. This led to their notion of "deferring judgment,"[46] which was in no sense the same as value-neutrality—more the approach of an artist like Ed Ruscha, whose deadpan photographs of the commercial Strip they greatly admired—nor for that matter of Pop reportage—the innovation of a "New Journalist" like Tom Wolfe, whose writing (in particular his early riff "Las Vegas (What?)...," published in 1964) was also inspirational but not a style they emulated. In other words, the Venturis never shed their pedagogical posture and missionary ambitions, even after leaving academia in the 1970s to concentrate on their practice. Moreover, if judgment deferral was a "heuristic technique"[47] that meant keeping an open mind with respect to the *déclassé* taste-culture of Las Vegas, it by no means kept them from being judgmental with respect to what they perceived as the architectural and intellectual establishment's reflexive ideological biases. In this respect, the sincerity and authenticity (two more 1960s buzzwords) of Venturi and Scott Brown's educational project were indubitable, and even

Cover of original edition of *Learning from Las Vegas* by Robert Venturi, Denise Scott Brown, and Steven Izenour (1972).

rather old-fashioned in terms of the exuberance, earnestness, and, increasingly, defensiveness with they sought to justify their radical revisionism, as well as their perennial avant-gardism. Fundamentally, indeed, their famous argument for decorated sheds over ducks was a functionalist and ethical one: "Our thesis is that most architects' buildings today are ducks: buildings where an expressive aim has distorted the whole beyond the limits of economy and convenience.... [The billboard] is an easier, cheaper, more direct, and basically more honest approach..."[48]

Ultimately, the impact of the Venturis' architecturally guided tour of Las Vegas was twofold. On the one hand, they succeeded in launching a whole new topos into architectural discourse. While other architects, notably Charles Moore (another peripatetic tourist), also embraced popular and roadside American culture in the 1960s, and while the Venturis' affirmation of Pop values had been anticipated by the British avant-garde of the 1950s, their critique of modernist architectural culture proved definitive. A major problem remained, however: how to translate the raw material they had gathered in Las Vegas, and the theoretical insights they gleaned from it, into their own architecture? Often their work was an awkward hybrid—academic Pop. As Colin Rowe pointed out with respect to their competition project for the Yale Mathematics Building in New Haven (1970), the attempt on the part of sophisticated architects to affect being "dumb and ordinary"—the overlay of "supposed innocence and very great formalism"—was a conceit.[49]

But the second powerful impact that came out of *Learning from Las Vegas* was a new graphic and representational repertory. The problem of describing the flatness of urban signage, the sequential experience of highway space-time, and the dynamism of advertising gave rise to innovative techniques of mapping, diagramming, charting, cataloguing, and composite photography. Notably these were rationalist devices, often based on the grid (Koolhaas and his students would exploit many of the same devices in their analyses, although with a hint of parody or excessiveness missing in the Venturis' work). At the same time, the Venturis also devised imaginative "postmodernist" forms of representation, from their playfully pointed appropriation of images—for example, the photograph of the Big Duck from Peter Blake's book *God's Own Junkyard*—to pastiches like a Las Vegas tourist advertisement overlaid on an eighteenth-century map of Rome by Giovanni Battista Nolli.

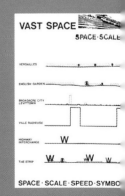

FROM COGNITIVE MAPPING TO GLOBAL POSITIONING

Blake's *God's Own Junkyard,* published in 1964, was yet another album of vivid black-and-white photography based on its author's road trips across the United States. Subtitled *The Planned Deterioration of America's Landscape,* it was a diatribe against America the Ugly ("This book is not written in anger. It is written in fury...").[50] In somewhat Mendelsohnian fashion, Blake, also a German émigré architect and critic although a generation younger, proceeded by juxtaposing images of good urbanism and bad, showing how Americans had fouled their once idyllic nest with billboards, cars, speculative real estate development, telephone poles, trash dumps, and other visual and environmental pollution.

The Venturis, with their *détournements* of Blake's images—not just the duck, but also other photographs from *God's Own Junkyard,* including views of Main Street and the commercial Strip, which they proclaimed "almost all right"—basically had the effect of reversing Blake's captions. It would remain for Rem Koolhaas, however, to take the Venturian strategy of devil's advocacy to its apocalyptic conclusion. Thus Blake's modernist-humanist indictment of the American junkscape would become Koolhaas's triumphalist revelation of the global junkspace.[51]

Indeed, Koolhaas's view of the world, from his early *Delirious New York* (1978) to the current Harvard series, provokes a strange sense of déjà-vu. On the one hand, there is a conscious and selective mining of pregnant ideas from the past century's most influential lineage of architect-tourists. On the other, their moral-political-critical content has been ruthlessly deconstructed and discarded, and their logic pushed to a point of either closure or farce. His recent work on commercial culture and urban mutations relates most explicitly to that of Venturi and Scott Brown, as he openly acknowledges (in oedipal fashion) in an interview with them included in his *Shopping* book, "Relearning from Las Vegas."[52] Yet their vision of Las Vegas now appears almost quaint in light of the new urban conditions he is describing, and their "social concern" is alien to his own concerns.

Opposite top, Robert Venturi (with W. G. Clark), project for MERBISC Mart, California City, California, 1970. "A standard small-scale strip, constructed according to local conventions with parking in front and service behind...a prediction rather than a design." Courtesy of Venturi, Scott Brown & Associates

Opposite bottom, "A comparative analysis of vast spaces." From Robert Venturi, Denise Scott Brown, and Steven Izenour, *Learning from Las Vegas.* Courtesy of Venturi, Scott Brown & Associates

Top, Big Duck roadside stand, Long Island, New York. Photo: Peter Blake. As published in Blake's *God's Own Junkyard* (1964) and reprinted in *Learning from Las Vegas*

Likewise, Koolhaas shares with his fellow Dutchman Van Eyck a fascination with Africa as civilizational other. But if Van Eyck sought timeless truths and universal values there, Koolhaas goes to the "dark continent" to find explicitly temporal ones. And if the older architect attempted to ground his gaze in humanistic anthropology, Koolhaas's gaze is overtly aestheticizing. Koolhaas has hinted that one of the roots/routes of his fascination with the traumatic unfolding of African and Asian modernization lies in his biography. Having spent four years of his childhood in Indonesia, from 1952 to 1956, when his father, a writer and film critic, took a position as head of a cultural institute in Jakarta, he has credited the experience of riding around the city in a chauffeur-driven car doing the family marketing in this colorful non-Western setting as a source of his subsequent interest in shopping.[53] Perhaps more significant for the formation of his attitude toward modern development, however, is the fact that these were particularly turbulent times in the newly decolonized republic. Three centuries of Dutch domination had finally come to an end in 1949, and the first half of the 1950s saw an unstable period of experimentation with liberal democracy under Sukarno, after which the revolutionary leader increasingly consolidated his power. More than 200,000 Dutch and Indo-Dutch fled the country during its initial decade of independence.

Koolhaas's colonial or postcolonial experience also evokes comparisons with Le Corbusier, another oedipal relationship that Koolhaas makes implicit in his treatment of the latter in *Delirious New York*.[54] With Le Corbusier Koolhaas shares—not without irony—the *veni, vidi, vici* of the monumental architectural ego, as well as a talent for publicity, a proclivity for publication, and a polemicizing avant-gardism. His early book on Manhattan (which, in its youthful exuberance and openness to experience, occupies a somewhat similar place in his career to *Voyage d'Orient* in Le Corbusier's) likewise contains a reverberation of Mendelsohn's New York books. Mendelsohn's celebration of the dynamism of the modern city, however, becomes Koolhaas's paean to delirium. In his more recent encounters with latter-day urbanism, Koolhaas sees himself, again somewhat like the German architect in the 1920s, as witness to the brutality and spectacle of history in the making.

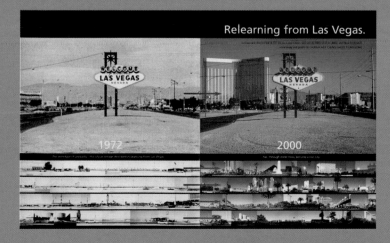

The Las Vegas Strip in 1972 compared to 2000. From *Harvard Design School Guide to Shopping* (2001)

But what sharply distinguishes Koolhaas's adventures from those of his predecessors is, as already suggested, his depoliticized or "postcritical" stance—a stance that in its reticence seems to harbor a very deep fear of such a form of engagement. It is not a matter of the Venturis' judgment deferral for the sake of greater receptivity, but rather an absolute refusal of anything that bears "soft" humanist residues. In a devolution from Mallarmé, one could almost say that Koolhaas's primary motivation for undertaking his various research projects is to have them end up as a (mega)book. And a further perversity: rather than allow the insights gleaned from his research to seep freely from the left side of his brain to the right, or from a conceptual phase into a representational one, Koolhaas has deliberately prised these two moments apart, as in his schizoid or "Siamese twin" construct of OMA/AMO. Thus, at the end of his film on Lagos, when the interviewer asks him if he would be willing to return to design something to help the city deal with its massive urban problems, he answers that that would entail a different kind of project. Similarly, in a dialogue in 2000 with the philosopher Cornel West, when West suggested that *inquiry* might be a term preferable to *research* (inasmuch as the former implies an ethically rather than instrumentally driven project, while the latter smacks of the values of the military-industrial-academic complex), Koolhaas passed over the suggestion without comment.[55]

As such, with Koolhaas we appear to have arrived at a paradigm shift. If we may characterize the objective that underlay the journeys of the most emblematic architect-tourists of the twentieth century as *cognitive mapping,* that of the globe-trotting Koolhaas (300 hotel nights a year) might be described as *global positioning.* The concept of cognitive mapping comes from Fredric Jameson, who in turn extracted and extrapolated it from the urban theorist Kevin Lynch, as articulated in a classic book of 1960, *The Image of the City.* There Lynch was concerned with the way people moving through a city make sense of their environment by constructing mental maps or itineraries. Lynch's primary preoccupation was legibility or "apparency," and the sense of disorientation and anxiety experienced by people when they lack an overall gestalt.[56] Lynch's approach was equally focused on perception and design: on educating urban citizens to be able to read visual and spatial cues in their environment, and on urban design as a discipline whose primary task was to produce "good"—i.e., comprehensible, unalienating—form.

Fully aware of the limitations of Lynch's anthropocentric, phenomenological-behaviorist approach, which not only spawned a dreary professional cadre of urban diagrammers in the 1960s but also lacked any conception of political agency or historical process, Jameson seized on it as a suggestive point of departure for his own postmodern theory of representation, focusing not just on city form but more broadly on the "social and global totality we all carry around in our heads in variously garbled forms."[57] Underpinning this reframing of Lynch's concept was Louis Althusser's (and Jacques Lacan's) seminal redefinition of ideology in positive terms, as a form of symbolic representation. For Jameson as for Althusser, the mapping "of the subject's Imaginary relationship to his or her Real conditions of existence"[58] was a necessary and inescapable human activity. It was precisely the gap between Lynch's physical, existential experience of the city and "a reality that

transcends all individual thinking or experience" that Jameson's cognitive map "of a new and global type" was designed to span or coordinate. But there was an equally important corollary for Jameson: just as the citizen's incapacity to map the city led to crippling disorientation, so the incapacity to map the "global totality" defeated the possibility, in his Marxian view, of any progressive political praxis. Thus, he concluded, cognitive mapping was in reality "nothing but a code word for 'class consciousness'" and its spatial representations.[59]

Inasmuch as Jameson's concept of cognitive mapping is to be understood, then, specifically as a political theory, it may also be seen more broadly as coeval with the reformist project of modernism. As such it underwrites the respective quests of each of the twentieth-century architect-tourists we have considered, with the ambiguous exception of Koolhaas. For Le Corbusier, Mendelsohn, Van Eyck, and the Venturis, a new way of seeing and its privileged mode of representation, whether drawing, photography, or literally mapping, was an instrument not just for theorizing the world but for ameliorating it. With Koolhaas, the gaze—strategic, media-savvy, inflated with *Zeitgeist*—remains arrested at the first stage of development, at least polemically, and wary of the second. It thus transforms "research" into an aesthetic, making an instrument into an end in itself.

Koolhaas's theoretical position may, of course, be taken as a symptom of the depth of his modernist disillusionment, or else simply as "wicked" avant-garde hyperbole. Surely his recent public buildings in Chicago, Seattle, and Oporto reflect a different vision, one a good deal more engaging, nuanced, and—in the traditional sense—enlightened in relation to architecture's functions in contemporary society. Yet it is clear that as the global horizons of difference have receded in the onslaught of advanced capitalism, requiring ever more exotic "trips" to satisfy the tourist's appetite for new stimuli, the architect's gaze too has become more refractory to experiential mediations. Thus Koolhaas coolly surveys the contemporary global condition from a totalizing vantage point that confirms and celebrates it in advance as junkspace. In contrast, the modernist gaze was frequently naive and misguided, but there was no doubt where its heart was.

NOTES

1. Rem Koolhaas/Harvard Project on the City, et al., *Mutations* (Barcelona: ACTAR, 2001), 117.

2. Rem Koolhaas, "City of Exacerbated Difference©," in Harvard Design School Project on the City, *Great Leap Forward* (Cologne: Taschen, 2001), 27.

3. *Lagos/Koolhaas*, film written and directed by Bregtje van der Haak, produced by Sylvia Baan for Pieter van Huystee Film (The Netherlands, 2002).

4. Ibid.

5. Ibid.

6. John Urry, *The Tourist Gaze: Leisure and Travel in Contemporary Societies* (London: Sage Publications, 1990), 1.

7. See Walter Benjamin, "The Work of Art in the Age of Mechanical Reproduction," *Illuminations* (New York: Schocken, 1969), 240–41.

8. Michel Foucault, *The Birth of the Clinic: An Archaeology of Medical Perception* (London: Tavistock Publications, 1973), 39; cited in Martin Jay, *Downcast Eyes: The Denigration of Vision in Twentieth-Century French Thought* (Berkeley: University of California Press, 1994), 384.

9. Michel Foucault, "Adorno, Horkheimer, and Marcuse: Who Is a 'Negator of History'?" in *Remarks on Marx*, cited in Martin Jay, *Songs of Experience: Modern American and European Variations on a Universal Theme* (Berkeley: University of California Press, 2005), 400.

10. Le Corbusier, *Journey to the East*, edited and translated by Ivan Žaknić (Cambridge, Mass.: MIT Press, 1987), 9.

11. Ibid.

12. Ibid.

13. Ibid., 41.

14. Stanislaus von Moos, "Voyages en Zigzag," in Stanislaus von Moos and Arthur Rüegg, eds., *Le Corbusier before Le Corbusier* (New Haven: Yale University Press, 2002), 23–43. See also Adolf Max Vogt, "Remarks on the 'Reversed' Grand Tour of Le Corbusier and Auguste Klipstein," *Assemblage* 4 (October 1987), 38–51.

15. Le Corbusier, *Journey to the East*, 170–71.

16. See Le Corbusier, "L'Espace indicible" (1945), translated as "Ineffable Space" in *New World of Space* (New York: Reynal & Hitchcock), 7–9. José Quetglas has suggested that Le Corbusier may have

borrowed the phrase "eyes that do not see" from a popular Spanish saying, the other half of which is "heart that does not feel": *Ojos que no ven, corazón que no se siente;* I wish to thank Adrian Luchini for calling this to my attention.

17. On Le Corbusier's acquaintance with the writings of Mallarmé, see Francesco Passanti, "Architecture: Proportion, Classicism, and Other Issues," in von Moos and Rüegg, *Le Corbusier before Le Corbusier,* 88, n. 90.

18. Le Corbusier, *The Decorative Art of Today,* translated by James Dunnett (Cambridge, Mass.: MIT Press, 1987), 207. I am grateful to Mary McLeod for drawing my attention to this source as well as for a number of other suggestions regarding this section on Le Corbusier.

19. Le Corbusier, *Journey to the East,* 220, 234.

20. Le Corbusier, *Creation Is a Patient Search,* translated by James Palmes (New York: Frederick A. Praeger, 1960), 37. Italics in original.

21. See Robert Slutzky, "Aqueous Humor," special issue on Le Corbusier 1933–1960, *Oppositions* 19/20 (Winter/Spring 1980), 30.

22. See, for example, Zeynep Celik, "Le Corbusier, Orientalism, Colonialism," *Assemblage* 17 (1992), 58–77; and Beatriz Colomina, "Battle Lines E.1027," in Diana Agrest et al., *The Sex of Architecture* (New York: Harry N. Abrams, 1996), 167–82.

23. Le Corbusier, *Précisions sur un état présent de l'architecture et de l'urbanisme* (Paris: G. Crès, 1930), n.p.

24. As Mardges Bacon has argued in her book *Le Corbusier in America: Travels in the Land of the Timid* (Cambridge: MIT Press, 2001). Bacon writes that the American experience changed Le Corbusier's outlook in important ways, among them giving him a more pragmatic view of industrial systems and techniques.

25. Jean-Louis Cohen, *Scenes of the World to Come: European Architecture and the American Challenge, 1893–1960* (Paris: Flammarion, 1995); see Hubert Damisch's preface, 8.

26. Gertrude Stein, "Why I Do Not Live in America," *Transition,* Fall 1928; reprinted in Stein, *How Writing Is Written,* ed. Richard Bartlett Haas (Los Angeles: Black Sparrow Press, 1974).

27. See Cohen, "The Eye of Mendelsohn," in *Scenes of the World to Come,* 85–98.

28. El Lissitzky, "Glaz Arkhitektora," *Stroitelnaya promyshlennost* 2 (1926), cited in Kathleen James, *Erich Mendelsohn and the Architecture of German Modernism* (Cambridge: Cambridge University Press, 1997), 68.

29. Thorstein Veblen, "Pecuniary Canons of Taste," in *The Theory of the Leisure Class* (New York: Penguin Books, 1979; orig. 1899), 154. Veblen's comment is in the same vein as Le Corbusier's injunction in *Vers une architecture* to imitate the work of American engineers, not American architects.

30. Guy Debord, *The Society of the Spectacle,* translated by Donald Nicholson-Smith (New York: Zone Books, 1995), 24.

31. "Mission Dakar-Djibouti, 1931–1933," *Minotaure* 2 (June 1, 1933).

32. I am indebted for a number of the details in this account to Karin Jaschke, who generously shared with me portions of her forthcoming dissertation, *Aldo van Eyck: Elements of a Complex Humanist Architecture.* See also Jaschke's essay "Architects in the Field: The African Journeys of Aldo van Eyck and Herman Haan," *Thesis* 1, vol. 49 (Bauhaus-Universität Weimar, January 2003).

33. Earlier fragments appeared in the American magazine *Architectural Forum* (September 1961) and the Dutch journal *Forum* (July 1967). The *VIA* material was reprinted in 1976 by the Eidgenössische Technische Hochschule, Zurich, under the title *Miracles of Moderation.*

34. Jaschke, manuscript of dissertation, part 3, note 3, and personal correspondence with author.

35. As published in S[igfried] Giedion, *Architecture, You and Me: The Diary of a Development* (Cambridge, Mass.:

Harvard University Press, 1958), 96.

36. *Forum* 7 (1959), 248.

37. Aldo van Eyck, *The Child, the City, and the Architect,* manuscript, 200; cited in Jaschke, part 3, 29.

38. On Rudofsky and *Architecture without Architects,* see Felicity D. Scott, "Bernard Rudofsky: Allegories of Nomadism and Dwelling," in Sarah Williams Goldhagen and Réjean Legault, *Anxious Modernisms: Experimentation in Postwar Architectural Culture* (Cambridge, Mass.: MIT Press, 2000), 215–37; and Felicity Scott, "Revisiting Architecture without Architects," *Harvard Design Magazine,* Fall 1998, 69–72.

39. Bernard Rudofsky, *Architecture without Architects* (New York: Museum of Modern Art, 1964), n.p.

40. Marshall McLuhan, *Counter-Blast* (New York: Harcourt Brace & World, 1969), 64. McLuhan coined the term *global village* in *The Gutenberg Galaxy* (Toronto: University of Toronto Press, 1962), 31ff.

41. Cited by David Brownlee in "Form and Content," in David Brownlee, David G. DeLong, and Kathryn B. Hiesinger, *Out of the Ordinary: Robert Venturi Denise Scott Brown and Associates* (Philadelphia: Philadelphia Museum of Art, 2001), 37.

42. Robert Venturi, Denise Scott Brown, and Steven Izenour, *Learning from Las Vegas* (Cambridge, Mass.: MIT Press, 1972). An abridged and much cheaper revised edition; which appeared in 1977, was intended to make the book available to a larger readership.

43. Alison and Peter Smithson, "But Today We Collect Ads," *Ark* 18 (November 1956); reprinted in David Robbins, ed., *The Independent Group: Postwar Britain and the Aesthetics of Plenty* (Cambridge, Mass.: MIT Press, 1990), 186.

44. Denise Scott Brown, "Learning from Pop," *Casabella,* December 1971, 15.

45. Ibid., 17.

46. See ibid., 23.

47. Ibid.

48. Denise Scott Brown and Robert Venturi, "On Ducks and Decoration,"

Architecture Canada, October 1968, 48.

49. Colin Rowe, "Robert Venturi and the Yale Mathematics Building," *Oppositions* 6 (Fall 1976), 16.

50. Peter Blake, *God's Own Junkyard* (New York: Holt, Rinehart and Winston, 1964), 7.

51. See Rem Koolhaas, "Junkspace: The Debris of Modernization," in *Harvard Design School Guide to Shopping* (Cologne: Taschen, 2001), 408–21.

52. Ibid., 590–617.

53. See interview with Jennifer Sigler in *Index Magazine* (2000), http://www.indexmagazine.com/interviews/rem_koolhaas.shtml, 2.

54. "Europeans: Biuer! Dalí and Le Corbusier Conquer New York," in Rem Koolhaas, *Delirious New York: A Retroactive Manifesto for Manhattan* (New York: Monacelli Press, 1994; orig. 1978), 235–81.

55. This exchange took place at the conference "Things in the Making: Contemporary Architecture and the Pragmatist Imagination," Museum of Modern Art, November 2000.

56. Kevin Lynch, *The Image of the City* (Cambridge, Mass.: MIT Press, 1960), 1–13.

57. Fredric Jameson, *Postmodernism or, The Cultural Logic of Late Capitalism* (Durham, N.C.: Duke University Press, 1991), 415. Interestingly, Roland Barthes also proposed a more ramified reading of Lynch's theory in his essay "Semiology and Urbanism," in *The Semiotic Challenge,* translated by Richard Howard (New York: Hill and Wang, 1988), 193.

58. Louis Althusser, "Ideological State Apparatuses" (1970), cited in Jameson, *Postmodernism,* 51 and 415.

59. Jameson, *Postmodernism,* 418.

Rem Koolhaas lecturing on the Lagos project. Still from *Lagos/Koolhaas,* 2002

JULIAN ROSEFELDT
OKTOBERFEST

1996–99
Color photographs, 48 x 104 inches

An annual tourist attraction in Munich, Oktoberfest is
the occasion for the erection of temporary architecture
on an enormous scale. Each "beer tent" hosts up to
7,000 drinkers in the ambiance of a vast artificial
pleasure garden.

CONTRIBUTORS

ACKBAR ABBAS is chair of comparative literature and co-director of the Center for the Study of Globalization and Cultures at Hong Kong University. His book *Hong Kong: Culture and the Politics of Disappearance* was published by University of Minnesota Press in 1997.

MARC AUGÉ is a social and cultural anthropologist. He was formerly director of the Ecole des Hautes Etudes en Sciences Sociales in Paris. Among his books in English are *Non-Places* (Verso, 1995), *The War of Dreams* (Pluto, 1999), and, most recently, *In the Metro*, from University of Minnesota Press (2002).

ANETTE BALDAUF is a cultural critic based in Vienna and New York. Her work focuses on feminism, pop culture, consumerism, and urbanism.

PELLEGRINO D'ACIERNO is a professor of comparative literature and director of the program in Italian Studies at Hofstra University. He is the editor of *The Italian-American Heritage* (Garland, 1999) and translator of *The Sphere and the Labyrinth* by Manfredo Tafuri (MIT Press, 1987). He is currently working on a book on architecture and film entitled *Strange Loops.*

DILLER + SCOFIDIO is a multidisciplinary design practice based in New York. Elizabeth Diller is a professor of architecture at Princeton University. With her partner, Ricardo Scofidio, she is the author of *Back to the Front: Tourisms of War*, published by Princeton Architectural Press in 1994. Among the major current projects of the firm, now known as Diller Scofidio + Renfro, are a new building for the ICA in Boston, the master plan for renovations to Lincoln Center in New York, and the competition-winning High Line in New York.

KELLER EASTERLING is an associate professor of architecture at Yale University. The author of *Organization Space: Landscapes, Highways, and Houses in America* (MIT Press, 1999), she is currently completing a new book entitled *Enduring Innocence: Global Architecture and Its Political Masquerades.*

TIM EDENSOR teaches in the cultural studies department at Staffordshire University, England. His *Tourists at the Taj* was published by Routledge in 1998. His most recent book is *National Identity, Popular Culture and Everyday Life* (Berg, 2002).

HANS HAACKE is a German-born conceptual and political artist who lives and works in New York. His work explores the ideological underpinnings of political and cultural institutions, confronting issues of corporate sponsorship, art patronage, and public representation.

CHRISTIANE HERTEL is a professor of art history at Bryn Mawr College. She is the author of *Vermeer: Reception and Interpretation* (Cambridge University Press, 1996). She is currently working on a book entitled *Critical Ornament/Ornamental Critique*, part of which deals with the modern and contemporary reconstruction of eighteenth-century German monuments.

MARK JARZOMBEK directs the History, Theory and Criticism in Architecture and Art program at Massachusetts Institute of Technology. His most recent book is *The Psychologizing of Modernity, Art, Architecture, and History* (Cambridge University Press, 2000).

SILVIA KOLBOWSKI is a conceptual artist and art critic living in New York. Formerly an editor of *October*, she is on the architecture faculty of Parsons School of Design.

D. MEDINA LASANSKY teaches architectural and urban history at Cornell University. She wrote her doctoral dissertation on Fascist architecture and urban spectacle. Her book *Architecture and Tourism: Perception, Performance and Place*, coedited with Brian McLaren, was published by Berg in 2004.

LUCY R. LIPPARD is a writer, activist, and curator living in Galisteo, New Mexico. She has been writing about contemporary art since 1964. Her recent book, *On the Beaten Track: Tourism, Art, and Place*, were published by New Press in 1999.

NEIL LEACH teaches architectural history and theory at the University of Bath in England. Among his books are *The Anaesthetics of Architecture* (MIT Press, 1999), *Millennium Culture* (Ellipsis, 1999), and, most recently, *The Human Chameleon* (MIT Press, 2002).

KARAL ANN MARLING is a professor of art history and American Studies at the University of Minnesota. Her books include *George Washington Slept Here* (Harvard, 1988), *The Colossus of Roads: Myth and Symbol along the American Highway* (University of Minnesota, 1984), and *Graceland: Going Home with Elvis* (Harvard, 1996). She edited *Building Disney's Theme Parks: The Architecture of Reassurance* (Canadian Centre for Architecture/Flammarion, 1997).

JOAN OCKMAN is an architectural historian and critic. She has directed the Temple Hoyne Buell Center for the Study of American Architecture at Columbia University since 1995. Among the books she has edited are *Out of Ground Zero: Case Studies in Urban Reinvention* (Prestel, 2002) and *Architecture Culture 1943–1968* (Rizzoli, 1993).

MARK ROBBINS was named dean of the School of Architecture at Syracuse University in 2004. He was formerly curator of architecture at the Wexner Center for the Arts and design director of the National Endowment for the Arts.

JULIAN ROSEFELDT is an artist living in Berlin. Trained as an architect, he frequently collaborates with Piero Steinle. Their work has been exhibited in the United States at PS1, New York; and Yerba Buena Center for the Arts, San Francisco. Among Rosefeldt's recent projects is *Asylum*, a multimedia work exploring themes of exoticism and stereotyping in relation to different immigrant groups.

MARTHA ROSLER is an artist living in Brooklyn, New York. Since the late 1960s, her work, which often combines images and texts, has been concerned with social issues. The catalog of her career retrospective, *Martha Rosler: Positions in the Life World,* was published in 1999, and a collection of 25 years of her writings, *Decoys and Disruptions,* appeared in 2003, both from MIT Press.

FELICITY D. SCOTT is an assistant professor of art history at the University of California, Irvine, and coeditor of the journal *Grey Room.* She is currently completing a book based on her doctoral dissertation on a proto-architourist, the Viennese architect Bernard Rudofsky.

PIERO STEINLE is a German artist currently living in Italy. Trained as an architect, he frequently collaborates with Julian Rosefeldt. Among Steinle and Rosefeldt's best-known installations exploring spatial fantasies and architectural themes are *Les Cathédrales Inconnues* (1995) and *Detonation Deutschland* (1996).

MITCHELL SCHWARZER is the chair of Visual Studies at California College of the Arts. He is the author of *German Architectural History and the Search for Modern Identity* (Cambridge University Press, 1995), *Architecture + Design: SF* (Understanding Business, 1998), and *Zoomscape: Architecture in Motion and Media* (Princeton Architectural Press, 2004). He is currently at work on a book entitled *Jewish Geographies.*

TEN ARQUITECTOS is based in Mexico City and New York. Principal Enrique Norten is a professor of architecture at the University of Pennsylvania. Besides the JVC Center for Guadalajara his current work includes a visual and performing arts library for the Brooklyn Public Library and Harlem Park, a tower in upper Manhattan.

BERNARD TSCHUMI ARCHITECTS has offices in New York and Paris. Among the firm's major buildings are the New Acropolis Museum in Athens, the School of Architecture at Florida International University, and Parc de la Villette in Paris. Bernard Tschumi is the author of the *Event Cities* series (MIT Press, 1994, 2001, 2005). He served as dean of the Graduate School of Architecture, Planning and Preservation at Columbia University from 1988 to 2003.

TSENG KWONG CHI, born in Hong Kong in 1950, was a photographer whose best-known work explores iconic tourist sites through the persona of an enigmatic Asian "emissary." A member of the avant-garde art scene in New York through the 1980s, he died of AIDS in 1990.

YI-FU TUAN is one of the founders of the field of human geography and a professor emeritus at the University of Wisconsin, Madison. A twenty-fifth anniversary edition of his book *Space and Place: The Perspective of Experience* was published by University of Minnesota Press in 2001. Among his other books are *Topophilia* (Columbia University Press, 1990) and *Escapism* (Johns Hopkins, 2000).

McKENZIE WARK is a critic living and working in New York. He was previously associated with the department of media studies at Macquarie University, Australia. Co-editor of the NetTime anthology *Readme!,* he is the author of *Virtual Geography: Living with Global Media Events* (Indiana University Press, 1993), *The Virtual Republic: Australia's Culture Wars of the 1990s* (Allen & Unwin, 1998), *Celebrities, Culture and Cyberspace* (Pluto, 1999), and *Dispositions* (Salt, 2002). His *Hacker Manifesto* was published by Harvard in 2004.

JAMES E. YOUNG is a professor of English and Judaic Studies at the University of Massachusetts Amherst, where he is also chair of the department of Judaic and Near Eastern Studies. Among his books are *The Texture of Memory* (1993) and *At Memory's Edge: After-Images of the Holocaust in Contemporary Art and Architecture* (2000), both published by Yale University Press. He recently served on the World Trade Center Memorial jury.

Front endpaper: Martha Rosler, photo of Norman Foster's Reichstag dome, Berlin, 2002.

Pages 2–3: Martha Rosler, photo of Charles de Gaulle Airport, Paris. From *In the Place of the Public: Airport Series,* ongoing.

Pages 4–5: Silvia Kolbowski, still from DVD *Something for Nothing,* 1996.

Pages 5–6: Julian Rosefeldt, from the photographic series *Oktoberfest,* 2002.

Page 8: Madelon Vriesendorp, "metaphorical analysis" of the Guggenheim Museum Bilbao. From Charles Jencks, *The New Paradigm in Architecture* (2002)

Page 61: InterContinental Resort Hotel Berchtesgaden, Obersalzberg, Germany, designed by Herbert Kochta, 2005.

Pages 86–87: Piero Steinle, still from audiovisual installation *Island,* 2002.

Page 103: The Hong Kong skyline seen from the West Kowloon Cultural District site. Photo: Alex Hofford, European Press Association

Pages 116–17: Universal CityWalk, Los Angeles, designed by Jon Jerde, 1993.

Pages 136–37: JVC Center, Guadalajara, Mexico, designed by TEN Arquitectos, 1998–.

Pages 190–91: Blur Building, Yverdon-les-Bains, Switzerland, designed by Diller + Scofidio, 2002.

Back endpaper: Piero Steinle, still from audiovisual installation *Island,* 2002.

© Prestel Verlag,
Munich · Berlin · London · New York

and The Trustees of Columbia University
in the City of New York, 2005

© of works illustrated by architects and artists, their heirs
or assigns, with the exception of works by Hans Haacke
by VG Bild-Kunst, Bonn 2005

Library of Congress Control Number: 2005903631

The Deutsche Bibliothek holds a record of this publication
in the Deutsche Nationalbibliografie; detailed
bibliographical data can be found under http://dnb.ddb.de

Prestel Verlag
Königinstrasse 9
80539 Munich
Tel. +49 (89) 38 17 09–0
Fax +49 (89) 38 17 09–35
www.prestel.de

Prestel Publishing Ltd.
4, Bloomsbury Place
London WC1A 2QA
Tel. +44 (20) 73 23–5004
Fax +44 (20) 76 36–8004

Prestel Publishing
900 Broadway, Suite 603
New York, NY 10003
Tel. +1 (212) 995–2720
Fax +1 (212) 995–2733
www.prestel.com

Prestel books are available worldwide. Please contact
your nearest bookseller or one of the above addresses for
information concerning your local distributor.

Design: Brett Snyder
Copyediting: Stephanie Salomon
Research assistance: Sara Goldsmith
Editorial direction at Prestel: Angeli Sachs, Sandra Leitte
Production at Prestel: Matthias Hauer
Lithography: Reproline Mediateam, Munich
Printing and binding: Imago, China
Printed in China on acid-free paper

ISBN 3–7913–3297–X